REFLECTIONS
ON THE
WORLD
ECONOM
CRISIS

REFLECTIONS
ON THE
WORLD
ECONOMIC
CRISIS

ANDRE GUNDER FRANK

Professor of Development Studies, University of East Anglia

Hutchinson

London Melbourne Sydney Auckland Johannesburg

Hutchinson & Co. (Publishers) Ltd

An imprint of the Hutchinson Publishing Group

24 Highbury Crescent, London N5 1RX

Hutchinson Group (Australia) Pty Ltd
30–32 Cremorne Street, Richmond South, Victoria 3121
PO Box 151, Broadway, New South Wales 2007

Hutchinson Group (NZ) Ltd
32–34 View Road, PO Box 40 086, Glenfield, Auckland 10

Hutchinson Group (SA) (Pty) Ltd
PO Box 337, Bergvlei 2012, South Africa

First published in Great Britain 1981

© Andre Gunder Frank 1981

Printed in the USA

British Library Cataloguing in Publication Data
Frank, Andre Gunder
   Reflections on the world economic crisis.
   1. Economic history — 1945–
   2. World politics — 1975–1985
   I. Title
   330.9'048   HC59

ISBN 0 09 144990 1 cased
     0 09 144991 X paper

CONTENTS

Preface

1. Reflections on the World Economic Crisis   7

2. World Crisis and Latin America's
   International Options   17

3. Economic Crisis, Third World, and 1984   23

4. World Crisis and Underdevelopment   39

5. Imperialism, Crisis, and Superexploitation
   in the Third World   53

6. The Economics of Crisis
   and the Crisis of Economics   66

7. Equating Economic Forecasting
   with Astrology Is an Insult—
   to Astrologers   104

8. World Crisis Theory and Ideology   111

9. Let's Not Wait for 1984:
   Discussion of the Crisis
   Andre Gunder Frank and Samir Amin   143

Notes   163

PREFACE

This book brings together some of my lectures and essays on the present world economic and political crisis dating from 1972 to 1980, as well as a long interview made jointly with Samir Amin, with whom I have had large areas of agreement about this crisis, in 1974. All of these pieces were originally intended for students and general readers who had no special economic or other professional training and who were hardly aware of the depth of the crisis before the mid-1970s. Therefore, these ideas should now be all the more comprehensible to general audiences, whose own experience in the meantime has made them increasingly aware of the development of this world crisis. Some of the material in the later chapters is based on my recent research; a more technical and extensive presentation is contained in my two longer books, *Crisis: In the World Economy* and *Crisis: In the Third World,* published in 1980 and 1981, respectively, by Holmes & Meier in New York and Heinemann in London.

The publication of these lectures and essays in a single volume necessarily involves some repetition of the central thesis, especially with regard to the place of the economic crisis of the industrial capitalist countries in the world economy. For present purposes, however, I have cut or otherwise revised some of the original pieces in order to avoid undue repetition of detail. On the other hand, the assembly here of the chapters in the chronological order of their delivery usefully reveals the evolution of one observer's perceptions of and reflections on the crisis step by step with its real development. Therefore this book also offers something of a sociology of knowledge (at least by one student) of the development of this world crisis

1

and its economic, social, political, ideological, and theoretical manifestations between 1972 and 1980.

The first chapter, announcing the development of a capitalist crisis of capital accumulation, is a lecture delivered in Rome in 1972, when the existence or even the threat of such a crisis was hardly yet perceived by anyone. With later hindsight the indications of the development of this crisis *could* have been observed from the mid-1960s, although some economists and politicians still have not seen them today. Before the 1973–1975 recession, the manifestations of the developing crisis were hardly visible to the untrained eye of the general public, or even the trained eye of most professional economists. Paul Samuelson, the world's foremost Keynesian economist, author of the most widely studied economics text, winner of the Nobel Prize in economics, and economic advisor to presidents, maintained as late as 1970 that Keynesian economic theory and policy had converted the prewar business cycle dinosaur into a postwar lizard that virtually eliminated recessions. As a nearly solitary voice in the wilderness (along with my friends Ernest Mandel, Giovanni Arrighi, Bob Sutcliffe, Andrew Gwyn, and very few others) in 1972, it should come as no surprise that my analysis of the crisis was still relatively vague and partial. But I believe it is a useful exercise to read these early reflections here and now.

The second chapter was prepared for a symposium on Latin America held in London in early 1974 under the sponsorship of the Royal Institute of International Affairs, with the participation of a Latin American ambassador and representatives of the international financial press. In contrast to them, I outlined some of the probable exploitative and repressive consequences that the crisis in the metropolitan capitalist countries would have in Latin America in particular and in the Third World in general. I regret to say that—as the reader can now verify—my somber predictions have been more than fully borne out by subsequent developments. Moreover, this conference took place shortly after the outbreak of the petroleum crisis in October 1973, when politicians and publicists the world over hastened to blame the "OPEC oil sheikhs" for all manner of economic difficulties and particularly for the beginnings of the 1973–1975 recession. By contrast, I insisted then and there that the economic crisis was much deeper and had other causes, and that the oil crisis was more the consequence than the cause of the real general crisis.

The third chapter is a combination of two lectures. The first was delivered at the International Congress of Sociology in Toronto, Canada, in August 1974 and concentrated on the political and economic problems generated by the crisis of capital accumulation in the West, with some references to the socialist countries of Eastern Europe. The second was delivered at the University of Papua New Guinea in Port Moresby in July 1975 and therefore placed greater emphasis on the prospects for the Third World in the current international crisis. The two lectures were consolidated into a single article, which was published in *World Development* in 1976 and is reprinted here. By the time of the Port Moresby conference, the gravity of the crisis had become abundantly evident—there were more than 15 million registered unemployed in the industrial economies and rates of inflation ranged from 10 to 25 percent a year. The attribution of the recession, and the crisis in general, solely or even primarily to the price of oil was no longer very plausible, and an increasing number of politicians and publicists were beginning to appeal to other arguments to justify the austerity policies that their populations were asked to accept without much resistance or complaint. Some personalities, like US Secretary of State Henry Kissinger and West German Chancellor Helmut Schmidt, began to speculate about the danger of another depression like that of the 1930s. Yet with the recovery after mid-1975, these fears began to disappear and were replaced by renewed optimism. The recession was a short-lived bad dream that had supposedly been caused by a unique combination of "external shocks"— like oil prices and bad harvests—which would not recur and could therefore be safely forgotten. Like hope, unfounded optimism and ostrich-like behavior seem to spring eternal. The long recovery until 1979 seemed to justify this hope for many, but not for the present writer. On the other hand, the continuing weakness of the recovery in investment and employment in the metropolitan economies (indeed, unemployment continued to grow during the "recovery" in Europe, Japan, Canada, and Australia) and the deterioration of the balance of payments in the peripheral economies also gradually undermined this hope for others and sowed increasing confusion among economists and politicians.

The fourth chapter is a transcription of a lecture which I delivered in the Netherlands, at the Catholic University in Tilburg, in October 1976. It begins with a review of the then current economic development and political manifestations of the crisis, particularly in the Third World, and attempts to explain them by analyzing how the crisis of accumulation has led to the imposition of austerity policies in the industrial capitalist countries and to accelerated differentiation, growing economic exploitation, and increased political repression in the Third World. The discussion examines the economic imperatives and political feasibility of pursuing austerity policies in the industrial countries and also refers to the growing participation of the socialist countries in the capitalist international division of labor.

Despite the recovery from the 1973–1975 recession, I continued my research on the further development and deepening of the crisis. The fifth chapter is a lecture delivered at the University of Barcelona in May 1977; it draws on my ongoing research into the superexploitation in the Third World as the counterpart of its new export promotion, particularly of manufactured goods. In the emerging international division of labor, low-wage exports from the Third World are intended to reduce costs of production and support profitability for international capital domiciled in the metropolitan countries. The same chapter also reviews the ideology and doctrine of "national security" that Third World military and authoritarian regimes have been invoking to legitimate their increased exploitation and repression.

Chapter 6 returns to the industrial capitalist countries. It was originally drafted (but subsequently not used) in 1976 as the first two chapters of my longer *Crisis* books. As subsequently edited and published by the editors of *Critique,* this chapter examines the bankruptcy of economic forecasters, who had been completely unable to foresee the 1973–1975 recession or the limitations to the recovery. It also examines the ineffectiveness of Keynesian economic policy and its demand managers, who were completely helpless in the face of the recession, except to promote it further, and inactive in the recovery, except to restrain it. Subsequently, economic events and the December 1977 meetings of the American Economic Association led *Business Week* to a similar evaluation, as it wrote in its issue of January 16, 1978, that the "economics profession faced intellectual bankruptcy . . . as the niggardly old-maidish science is increasingly concerned with arranging and rearranging old furniture . . . and the Administration's statements about the economy had been so vague that they had the character of a Greek oracle." Chapter 7, written in early 1979, documents the extreme extent to which not only vague but downright contradictory government statements about the economy had become the rule throughout 1977. US Secretary of the Treasury Michael Blumenthal, for instance, predicted within one month's time that at least three years of prosperity lay ahead and that the then current upturn would not last. After his resignation from public office, Mr. Blumenthal said that "the people running the major economies of the world don't know what they are doing. . . . Of all the economic projections we got on growth and unemployment—and we consulted a wide spectrum—not a single one turned out to be right" (*Financial Times,* October 19, 1979). This was telling commentary on the best that orthodox, professional economic forecasting and high-level economic policymaking have had to offer in the face of the ever deepening world crisis.

This same theme is taken up again on a much broader canvas in Chapter 8, which combines an essay and a lecture from mid-1979 that were revised in 1980. It reviews both the development of the real, international economic and political crisis and the associated crisis in economic theory, political ideology, and social policy in each sector of the world and in current political philosophies tendencies, from the reactionary right through the social democratic center to the Marxist left. This chapter summarizes many of the findings presented at length in my longer books on the crisis and explores some of their implications at a time when President Carter is lamenting the national "crisis of confidence," the World Bank and other international institutions foresee growing poverty in the Third World, and the leading socialist and self-reliant countries "teach others a lesson" by invading their neighbors to change their governments or political policies.

The final piece is the first English translation of a very lengthy joint interview of Samir Amin and myself, first published in Italian in *Il Manifesto* in February 1974 and subsequently translated into various other languages. The interview ranged widely over many of these problems. Already in 1974 we reviewed, and, in alternate fantasies of Orwell's *1984,* previewed developments in various parts of the world in crisis. Our messasge in 1974, as now, was "Let's not wait for 1984" to do something about it!

Andre Gunder Frank
Norwich, England

June 1980

1. REFLECTIONS ON THE WORLD ECONOMIC CRISIS

Since 1970, though the roots go further back than that, there has been a new crisis of capital accumulation in the imperialist camp. One could perhaps discuss whether this crisis is most similar to the one in 1873, the first so-called great crisis. One of the important things which became evident at that time was that it was possible to increase the wage level in industrialized, metropolitan countries in spite of, or even as an integral part of, the crisis. As Alonso Aguilar noted yesterday, however, this was done at the cost of the growing exploitation of the labor force in the colonies and neocolonies associated with imperialist penetration. Or perhaps the crisis is more like the world crisis in 1929. At that time, at least in some colonial and neocolonial countries, what then seemed to be a more autonomous capitalist development began; yet this was later revealed to be nothing but a sort of repetition of previous dependent development. In other words, the first kind of dependent development, focussed on raw material extraction, followed the 1873 crisis, while another form of development came with the last crisis and centered around an industrial pole. The third possibility would be to discuss this current crisis as more than a major cyclical crisis, but also as a long-term structural crisis of the capitalist process of capital accumulation. In addition to having cyclical features, the crisis may bring with it transformations unknown up to now and perhaps still not adequately

---

This is a revised version of a speech presented in Spanish at the Conference of Latin American and Italian Social Scientists, organized by the Institute for Study of Contemporary Society (ISSOCO), in Rome, September 1972. Some references to statements by other participants have been omitted. It was translated by Mimi Keck.

analyzed because we are only at the beginning of this great crisis.

However you want to look at it, a series of features of the current crisis more or less jumps out at you: the relative decline of production, the decline of profits and investments, and the resulting renewed struggle over markets. One of the ways this was expressed was in last year's [1971] financial crisis. Even the United Nations Conference on Trade and Development secretariat recognized that this was primarily a financial crisis motivated by a struggle over markets, developing through changes in exchange rates and currencies, with the goal being to win and hold onto more markets than one's rivals.

Another more or less clear expression is the resurgence or strengthening of economic blocs. After twenty years of what for some seemed to be an age of superimperialism, there has been a tendency toward a renewed strengthening of economic blocs, like the United States and Latin America, Western Europe with its backyard in Africa, and Japan's renewed expansion, similar to its Greater East Asian Co-prosperity Sphere of the 1930s. This leaves undefined for the moment an area represented primarily by Asia and perhaps by part of the Middle East. It is interesting to note that in the two previous crises there was a marked tendency toward the strengthening or formation of economic blocs; classical colonialism was one expression of this. The same can be said of the policies which Joan Robinson and others call "beggar-my-neighbor," the attempt to make one's neighbor pay the costs of the crisis. With the development of fascism in Europe, a large part of Eastern Europe was similarly used as a backyard for the imperialist powers.

As in the past, it also appears that the greatest qualitative changes in the international division of labor occur during a period of crisis in capital accumulation, and that these changes are then quantitatively extended during a following period of expansion, which has been facilitated by these changes. Such upswings evidently took place after previous crises; it remains to be seen whether the present crisis will also be followed by an expansion.

I would like to stress the fact that even though quantitatively these changes in the international division of labor are most visible during the ascending periods of the great cycle, qualitatively they seem to be concentrated at the moment of crisis and in the first years of downturn. It is then that a major struggle over markets takes place, a struggle that is also based on a relative change in the productive forces between one economic power and another, as happened at the end of the last century. These new qualitative changes in the international division of labor are, of course, seen most clearly in Europe and Japan.

One aspect of these changes is the development of sub-imperialism, as Ruy Mauro Marini analyzed it with reference to Brazil. But the Brazilian case must not be seen as something unique: we could also study the subimperialist development of South Africa. Indeed, it has been said that Brazilian and South African subimperialism behave like allies at the same time as they behave like competitors in Africa. Evidence of South African subimperialism can be seen in what is called the "dialogue" in Africa, which first took place between South Africa and Dr. Hastings Banda of Malawi and, later, with Mouphouët-Boigny of the Ivory Coast. We can suppose that this will happen more and more with other African countries, even those where, up to two or three years ago, the idea of entering into a dialogue with the South African racist government was unthinkable. Nevertheless, today they are doing it, in part on their own account, in part not. In the case of the Ivory Coast, which is nothing but a neocolony (hardly that, for it is practically a colony of France), it is clear that its interest in South African subimperialism can only be the interest of France and perhaps of the whole European Economic Community. In this perspective, it can be seen as the cutting edge, as an instrument with which to confront US imperialism in Africa, which (and I don't know if this could happen) could in turn carry on its activities through Brazilian subimperialism.

Other cases include the nascent subimperialism in Iran in the Middle East (even though Israeli subimperialism has been active there for a long time). The new and growing subimperialism in formative stages in India is important for the whole South Asian subcontinent, now that it has eliminated Pakistan as a rival in the same way that Brazil eliminated Argentina as a potential rival in its respective sphere. What is interesting about Indian subimperialism is its relation not only with the United States, but with the Soviet Union. The two powers would seem to be encouraging Indian subimperialism: although they are competitors, they also have common interests in the region, and Indian subimperialism could protect these.

Evidently the spread of the subimperialist phenomenon is due not only to the economic, political, and military interests of the imperialist powers or of the Soviet Union, but also to the development of the productive forces in each of those regional centers—India, Brazil, Israel, and so forth. In addition, there is growing interest on the part of the socialist countries, and especially the Soviet Union, in participating to a much greater degree and in a different way in the international division of labor, which is now undergoing these qualitative changes. The economic, diplomatic, and political offensive by the socialist countries must at least partly be interpreted as an attempt to take advantage of this conjuncture, and of the changing international division of labor. They do not want to be left out of the new positions which the different economic powers will have reached when this period of rapid change is over. All evidence points to the fact that this offensive on the part of the socialist countries stems in part from domestic causes, and is certainly also due to characteristics of socialist capital accumulation, which are insufficiently well understood.

It is interesting to note the similarity, perhaps superficial but perhaps not, between the role of the subimperialist powers in the international division of labor and that of some socialist countries, particularly the Soviet Union. In both cases, they import the most advanced technology possible from the imperialist centers: that is, they do not import the most advanced technology, because they cannot get access to it, but they import what we might call second-level technology, and they develop their industry using this. The products of that industry are then exported to poorer countries, whose productive forces are currently not developed enough to participate in the international division of labor at the same level. It is also interesting that the socialist countries have a growing balance of payments surplus with the underdeveloped countries: the underdeveloped countries run a deficit both with the imperialist countries and with the socialist countries, and the growing exchange with the socialist countries only serves to aggravate the underdeveloped countries' deficit.

The tendency is thus for the socialist countries to export raw material—especially fuel—to the imperialist countries, importing industrial products in turn. At the same time, they export manufactured goods to the underdeveloped countries, and import raw materials from them, but not the same ones they export to the imperialist nations. In reality, this is planned by the socialist countries themselves, as can be seen in the 1971 Comecon economic plan of the Council for Mutual Economic Assistance, in the national plans of different socialist countries, and in their public statements. Now, it is interesting to note that *Corriere della Sera* (I don't know whether it is a reliable source) said recently that last week's US-Soviet talks arrived at an agreement that implies an exchange between these two countries, for 1973 alone, amounting to $5 billion, equal to more than half of US exports to all of Latin America. In other words, we are talking about something significant, not just a secondary phenomenon within the international division of labor.

All this must have a political counterpart, what has come to be known on an international level as "detente." This was exemplified in the well-known Nixon trips. I would be inclined to say that the crisis in the imperialist countries has as a consequence—Ruy Mauro Marini might say that the consequence has a cause—the growing mobilization of the working class and its struggle for higher wages, or at least its struggle against the bourgeois imperialist governments' attempts to lower the wage rate. In the case of England, for example, this has been very visible. First the Labour government failed to come up with a law to restrain labor. The Conservative Party was voted in to make such a law and drew up the Industrial Relations Act. But in spite of major efforts, it has not up to now been able to enforce that law because of the exceptional resistance of the English trade unions, a level of resistance which has not been seen since perhaps the 1926 coal strike. Other European countries have also experienced growing working-class mobilization, which the bourgeoisie has attempted to contain, or to channel in a social democratic direction (borrowing the word "social democracy" from an earlier crisis).

I do not know if this implies—and this is what Mauro Marini seems to think—that, despite many differences, we are experiencing a crisis similar to the one of a century ago, which was not expressed by a decline in wages in the industrialized urban centers but therefore all the more so in the colonies and neocolonies. If this were true, it would indicate—though it is a little too soon to say—that social democracy will be on the agenda in the imperialist countries, as in the nomination of George McGovern as Democratic candidate for president in the United States, the popular front or even popular unity type of pact between François Mitterand and the French Communist Party, or what some have called "Chile with spaghetti sauce" in Italy. These would be, in other words, social democratic efforts, whose chances are difficult to predict, but they are accompanied by fascist responses in case social democratic efforts fail.

In the underdeveloped countries the crisis also shows up in growing mobilization, especially of the working masses. This is particularly the case in Latin America, but one can also point to analogous phenomena in South Asia, Bangladesh, Ceylon, to a certain extent in Indira Ghandi's India and even in Ali Butto's Pakistan, after his defeat in the war. Up to the present, this has also ended in a series of neosocial democratic attempts to form broad electoral fronts, as seen in Ecuador, Venezuela, Uruguay, in the electoral conduct in Chile until its victory in 1970, and in the resurgence of Peronism in Argentina. It is premature to voice an opinion about the prospects of these social democratic arrangements in the underdeveloped countries. In Ceylon they have already met with almost complete failure; in Bangladesh, though they are still very new, they are heading for defeat, and we can note a slow movement toward a kind of neofascism. This also appears very likely in India, to say nothing of Egypt and other countries in the Middle East. In Ecuador, electoral procedures were cut short by a coup. We can harbor some doubts about Venezuela, Argentina, and Uruguay. In summary, the tendency toward neofascist arrangements seems to be growing in the underdeveloped countries, particularly in the subimperialist nations—especially, of course, for the reasons Marini has given.

These alternatives would leave a margin for building a thesis—somewhat like Arghiri Emmanuel's, although that was erroneously derived from his analysis of unequal exchange—that the imperialist countries might be able to face the world crisis "successfully" by using social democratic means. This would be possible if they could make an appreciable part of the cost and financing of the recovery of the rate of profit fall back on the superexploitation of the underdeveloped countries and also of at least some of the socialist countries. However, and especially as the crisis grows deeper, we must bear in mind the danger that, in spite of the safety valve which the underdeveloped and socialist worlds represent for imperialism, and in spite of social democratic arrangements, or, better yet, because of the social democratic leadership of popular mobilization in the imperialist countries, the bourgeoisie may be presented with a fascist or neofascist option as the only way out of the crisis. This could happen with both the imperialist and the underdeveloped bourgeoisies—unless, of course, the working class has the political leadership necessary to open up a revolutionary and socialist solution.

Finally, then, under these circumstances we should not be surprised that dependency theory, as it was developed during the 1960s, is not at all adequate to understanding and confronting the new crisis of capital accumulation, which requires a return to the analysis of that process. It is natural that this should be happening now, as accumulation is once again in crisis. Like the business cycle, capital accumulation is studied only in its phase of decline, because in its phase of ascent no cycle is perceived, only a "natural" and "permanent" development upward. Then the study of the cycle passes out of fashion until the next crisis, when it becomes fashionable again. Thus we can understand why today there is a call for this kind of global analysis. It is a response not so much to theoretical gaps, which might have been found long ago because they were inherent in the theory of dependency, but to the political and ideological demands of the present situation in the world today.

The call for a study based on class structure and its dynamic in each country is also necessary in view of the renewed mass mobilization underway in the imperialist as well as the underdeveloped countries. Although dependency theory is dead, in reality it is alive, because there is no question of replacing it with a theory or ideology that negates dependency, but rather with one that goes beyond the limits of dependency theory to incorporate dependency and dependency theory into a global analysis of accumulation. This also implies the inadequacy of the kind of analysis—I would even call it ideology—coming from such sources as the orthodox, pro-Moscow Communist parties. In the imperialist countries they criticize dependency theories and then espouse a theory which on the one hand criticizes Wall Street-type monopolies, and the connections among them as separate entities, and on the other hand focuses on an apparent antifascist struggle, the claim being that fascism is only an occasional, extreme, and superficial aberration of capitalist society, a sort of nonmalignant tumor that can be extricated by a coalition policy of social democratic fronts. Furthermore, in the underdeveloped countries—in Latin America, but also in India, and perhaps elsewhere—the Communist parties also criticize dependency theory. But what they try to put in its place is nothing but an update of traditional policy of anti-imperialist, antioligarchical struggle in favor of a bourgeois democratic revolution. This, so to say, is the underdeveloped social democratic version of the same position but applied to the specific conditions of the underdeveloped, neocolonized countries. This Communist position is not a real critique of dependency theory; still less is it the needed substitute for dependency theory. In fact, it is nothing but the resurrection of the position (of the Third International) that these parties adopted during the last crisis, when it was obviously not very successful. In the current crisis, which has original characteristics, we can expect that this position will be destined to even greater failure.

Therefore we have to support the call for a global analysis of accumulation, and perhaps attempt to thoroughly analyze power politics. Finally, we must consider that this apparent choice between fascism and social democratic reformism is perhaps less a choice than two different forms of one single line of development in the crisis, in both the imperialist and subimperialist countries, in the underdeveloped and sub-imperialized ones. In this respect it is symbolically interesting to watch the attempt of Italian fascism to convert Peronism into a banner, given the fact that Peronism, though at the time it sometimes called itself fascist, has been interpreted for the last two decades in Latin America as a social democratic, reformist, bourgeois movement.

Particularly in the underdeveloped countries, and perhaps in the imperialist ones as well, we are beginning to understand that these categories (social democracy, fascism, etc.) were borrowed from the last crisis, and in some cases even from the one before that. They may no longer be adequate for the social form which the current crisis will take. It could combine elements of social democracy and fascism into a form that has been little known up to now and that could be nationalist-corporatist or neocommunist. We must emphasize the fact that in the underdeveloped countries developments will take, or have already taken, the form of wars, where most of the combatants act in the capacity of figureheads for other powers.

For revolutionaries, then, it will be important in the first place not to let ourselves be deceived by solutions that are not solutions, but rather to prepare ourselves and the mobilized masses, especially the working masses, to take advantage of the inevitable worsening of the crisis, and to avoid insofar as is possible both social democracy and fascism, or any combination of the two. And in those cases where the crisis generates an objectively revolutionary situation—which may happen in part with the help of those wars that José Augustín Silva was talking about—we must be able to take advantage of these crises and be in a position to make the socialist revolution. We must not once again lose the opportunity the last crisis presented in countries like France, Italy, and Greece; there, precisely because of the kind of strategy we have been criticizing, the opportunity was lost, and we have the world situation we live in today.

2. WORLD CRISIS AND LATIN AMERICA'S INTERNATIONAL OPTIONS

The international options of the countries of Latin America will depend in the future, as in the past, on the course of capitalist development in the remainder of the world, including internal political developments in the Latin American countries themselves. These in turn will depend largely on the nature and course of capitalist development in the world as a whole, as well as on the stage and kind of capital accumulation in each Latin American country. With respect to these economic and political developments during the 1970s, we may hazard the following working hypotheses. These summarize, however schematically, some of the contradictory tendencies of uneven capitalist development, which for the foreseeable future are likely to determine the international options and relations of Latin America in the 1970s.

Uneven capitalist development. World capitalist development appears to be entering upon another major crisis of capital accumulation analogous to, albeit not repetitive of, the period between 1873 and 1895, which witnessed the birth of monopoly capitalism and imperialism, and the period which included World War I and World War II and the intervening Great Depression. Whether or not such periods of more frequent and deeper cyclical crises of accumulation correspond to the quarter-century-long downswings of so-called long cycles

This is a revised version of a paper that was presented at a symposium on Latin America, sponsored by the Royal Institute of International Affairs in London, May 1974.

sometimes associated with the name of Kondratieff and others, the end of the long post–World War II upswing and the beginning of the current downswing may tentatively be dated from 1967, after which rates of profitability and of growth of investment in the major capitalist countries of North America, Europe, and Japan seem to have initiated a period of decline. The contemporary "stagflation," currency crises, and breathtaking changes in international political relations may be seen as symptoms of this growing crisis of accumulation. The same crisis forebodes increased temporal, spatial, and sectoral maladjustments, as well as a sharpening of the class struggle; and this at the same time will generate the opportunity and the necessity for major readjustments in world capitalist development, readjustments which will be necessary if capitalism is to overcome its present crisis instead of being destroyed by it and replaced by another social system. The international relations of the countries of Latin America, like those of the remainder of the world, will be largely determined by this process of maladjustment and readjustment in the coming years.

The international division of labor. The increased exhaustion of major investment opportunities and reduced rates of profit are likely to restrain the quantitative extension of the intersectoral and international division of labor in certain directions (such as runaway shops in textile and electronics parts industries to areas of cheap labor, if only because of political resistance by unions and others in the metropolitan economies). At the same time, the crisis of world capital accumulation is likely to generate deeper and faster qualitative changes in technological invention and in the intersectoral and international division of labor. The development of major new sources of energy (nuclear fusion, solar, and so forth), exploitation of the oceans and the ocean floor for minerals and "agricultural" products, and developments in biochemistry and genetics are likely to be among these major new directions. If and when profitability can again be enhanced through technological progress, reduction of the wage rate, and an increase in the rate of exploitation, the degree of capital intensity of capitalist production is likely to again increase. In these periods of accelerated maladjustment and readjustment, the development and exploitation of sources of raw materials appears to be more important relative to that of the production and trade of industrial commodities than it is during the decades of rapid capitalist economic growth, such as those preceding World War I and following World War II. In addition, the coming period may witness a transfer of the production of energy and certain minerals to the industrialized countries and "their" oceans, while these countries will in turn transfer some production, not only of textiles and electronic parts but also of steel and automobiles, to certain of the underdeveloped and socialist countries. These latter will be increasingly drawn into the international and intersectoral division of labor, with far-reaching consequences for their international and domestic economic and political relations.

Capitalist competition for monopoly and exploitation. The capitalists' attempt to turn the tide of declining profits and profitable investment opportunities during the crisis of accumulation increases competition for markets among them (a partial reflection of this is the currency crisis) and promises a revival of the "beggar-my-neighbor" policy of the previous major crisis. Of particular relevance for Latin America's options, it also induces them to intensify and accelerate the exploitation of some socialist and Third World economies through primitive (noncapitalist) accumulation and unequal exchange, while acceding to the greater participation in this same process by some intermediary economies and regimes. At the same time, to assure the greatest possible share of the pie for each of the major powers, it augurs the strengthening of economic blocs and monopolistic relations within the capitalist countries. This tendency will be increasingly strengthened by any further breakdown of the present dollar-based international currency system and the renewed formation of a dollar area, of Euro-currency or deutsche mark and French franc areas, a sterling area, a yen area—not to mention a ruble area. Increased multipolarity leads to detente and shifting alliances but also threatens major political conflict, including military confrontation, between some of the "allies," such as the USSR and China on the one hand, and Japan and its US and European partners on the other hand, if not directly, then indirectly in Third World countries.

Class struggle in the industrialized capitalist countries. The profit squeeze in the major capitalist countries implies not only an attempt to shift the burden of the costs onto other countries, but—especially insofar as the increased costs the workers in these countries will have to bear will be insufficient to stem and reverse the tide of the crisis of capital accumulation in the major capitalist countries—the workers in the major capitalist countries will be obliged to bear a substantial part of the sacrifices themselves. The sharpening of the class struggle, particularly in Western Europe, has been increasingly in evidence and promises to become still more extensive and intensive in the decade to come. A first response to this intensification of the class struggle is the revival of social democratic, labor, popular unity, or popular fronts in an attempt to share the burden of the crisis and to persuade labor to "sacrifice its selfish interests to the national interest in this time of crisis." The threatened failure of these social democratic "solutions" to the crisis, especially as it deepens internationally and nationally, will enhance and accelerate the threat of, and indeed pave the way for, recourse to neofascist corporative and even militarist solutions. The course of this class struggle in the major capitalist countries will, of course, also determine the economic, political, and ideological positions taken by their governments, as well as their foreign policies with respect to each other, the socialist countries, and the Third World countries, including those of Latin America. Needless to say, this will be all the more true if the bourgeoisie fails to find the resources to save capitalism in its next period of crisis and the working class finds the political means to overthrow that ruling class and replace capitalism by socialism.

The Third World in the present crisis. The accelerated qualitative transformation of the international division of labor during the present crisis of capitalist development offers increased opportunities for the development of intermediary, subimperialist economies and regimes along the Brazilian model and at the same time generates further pressures for the formation of increasingly dependent client states along the post-Allende Chilean model. Economies which achieved a certain level of development of their productive forces since the last major crisis of world capitalism, like India, South Africa, Brazil, and to a lesser extent Mexico and Argentina (and, albeit under socialism, the Soviet Union) will find new opportunities to advance their position in the international division of labor in new directions. Some other petroleum-producing countries and, to a lesser degree, Egypt and Algeria, will find the opportunity to acquire subimperialist status. This implies further capitalist development for those economies that permit a political alliance of their bourgeoisies with those in the imperialist nations, and with some sectors of their own middle class. However, especially for the former countries, unlike the import-substituting development of consumer goods industries based on an extension of the internal market, a more progressive income distribution, and a relatively progressive populist regime, all of which took place during the last world crisis of accumulation, the coming capitalist development of these economies is likely to rest increasingly on accumulation through capital goods and export industries, whose output must be bought by the external market, by industry itself, by high-income receivers, and particularly by the state, including its military apparatus. This implies (1) further regression in the distribution of income, (2) increased unemployment beyond the 25 percent "effective unemployment equivalent" estimated by the United Nations for Latin America for 1970, (3) low-wage policies, such as those that have reduced the wage rate in Brazil by 40 percent during the "economic miracle," (4) increased marginalization of large portions of the population, and (5) reactionary political regimes that pursue internal policies of repression, external policies of expansionism, militarism, and international political alliances with other reactionary regimes, while seeking to maintain a delicate and shifting balance of dependent autonomy in their international economic and political relations.

Despite the vain hopes of their political leaders, most countries in the Third World, including Latin America, cannot realistically aspire to such subimperialist development. In this crisis, as in past ones, the large masses of people will likely suffer from vastly intensified superexploitation and political repression. Here, as is the case in the Philippines and large parts of South Asia, the degree of superexploitation, unemployment, marginalization, and, of course, repression, threaten to go much farther—as they already have in Chile in half a year—than in the case of the subimperialist regimes, whose victims they are increasingly likely to become. For the corporatist, if not the military, state appears to be the order of the day, and the degree to which brutal repression will replace institutional repression will be a measure of the degree to which such corporatism has been achieved. In their international relations with the imperialist powers—and with some subimperialist ones—these repressive, neofascist, corporatist states are condemned to an even greater economic and political dependence than was the case in the past. And as for the relations among countries of the Third World and Latin America, there is the threat of growing cutthroat economic competition, as well as political confrontation and war. In the next deep crisis of capitalism, only the successful popular revolutionary overthrow of capitalism can avoid such human costs.

3. ECONOMIC CRISIS, THIRD WORLD, AND 1984

There is growing evidence that the world is again in crisis, a crisis analogous to others in recent history. There has been a lot of talk, increasing talk perhaps, about the end of an era, the end of the postwar world, the passage to a new era. Some of this evidence is that some years ago there was, first, a passage from bipolarity to multipolarity in the international political arena; then the currency crisis of 1970–1971, associated with a cyclical downturn in several of the industrial countries; then the oil crisis in 1973–1974 and the renewed cyclical depression, or cyclical recession, of 1974–1975, by far the most serious that the industrialized countries have known since the end of the war and, in a sense, since the 1930s.

I suggest that this mounting evidence, and other evidence to which I shall refer, adds up to the probability that the capitalist world is again in a serious crisis of accumulation, that is to say, a crisis in the process of capital accumulation. In part, one of the other symptoms is that the rate of profit in the major industrial countries seems to have declined, a process that began in the mid-1960s. For this reason one possible date of the beginning of the crisis might be placed at that time prior to the mounting evidence I referred to in the previous paragraph. There has been a decrease in the rate of profit on capital and a decrease in a number of important areas of profitable investment opportunity. There has also been an increase, known to most of us, in the monetization of the economy and an increase in the amount of credit, the first associated in large part with the inflation

This is a revised version of a paper that originally appeared in *World Development* 4: 853–861, 1976. It is reprinted here by permission of the publisher.

which the industrial countries, but not only the industrial countries, have experienced in recent years, far beyond any in recent memory. (I would suggest as an aside that this inflation reflects not simply an increase in the supply of money and credit but an attempt on the part of capital to stem the tide of falling profits by jacking up prices—and this of course is supported by the governmental monetary and capital authorities.) This is increasingly possible, in an increasingly monopolized economy, so that there can be a substantial rate of inflation and simultaneously a substantial underutilization of resources and substantial unemployment. In addition, the increase in credit, in the debt-equity ratio among corporations, and in private indebtedness are all attempts to avoid a total collapse of the economic system. Of course, to the extent that continued economic activity is based on an increasingly fragile credit structure, this postponement may—I cannot say that it will, but it has in past experience done so on several occasions— lead to a very serious crash, all the more serious by virtue of the construction of a sort of house of cards based on credit.

There is growing agreement along these lines among world leaders, industrialists, and bankers. Henry Kissinger, Harold Wilson, former prime minister of Great Britain, Helmut Schmidt, prime minister of West Germany, to name only a few, have all since 1974 made repeated references to the danger, the imminent danger as implied in some of their declarations, of a crash of the 1929 variety and of a depression analogous to that of the 1930s. They themselves do not recall, perhaps because as politicians their memories are not long or because the audiences to whom they speak do not have long memories, that the world passed through such crises not only in the 1930s, but also in the 1870s and 1880s, and in even earlier periods of world capitalist development. Moreover, although these gentlemen refer primarily to the depression of the 1930s, that was part and parcel (in one sense perhaps the culmination, in another sense not so much so) of a deep crisis in the capitalist accumulation of capital that lasted from 1914 to 1945 before giving way again to a long period of capitalist expansion that has come to be known as the postwar era of permanent growth—"permanent growth" that has now turned out to be not so permanent at all.

These periods of deep crisis in the process of capital accumulation have in the past brought with them important qualitative changes in the international and intersectoral divisions of labor, and as a result of important concomitant changes in the social and political structure in the world as a whole, they have sharpened intranational and international conflict. The last of these crises generated World War I and World War II, the depression between them, and the rise of fascism as a direct result of this depression—as well as the Soviet revolution, the Chinese revolution, and the apparent potential for socialist revolutions in France and Italy after 1945.

In the past these major crises of accumulation have not only necessitated, but have also rendered possible, a far-reaching qualitative change in the division of labor. The crisis itself means that the process of accumulation ("development" or "growth" are perhaps more popularly used terms, but are not quite the same thing) no longer functions as it has in the past and requires major readjustments in order to make it function again in the future. At the same time, the crisis makes these readjustments possible inasmuch as without the crisis there would be no reason, or no *pressing* reason, to undergo the far-reaching changes, often at very great social and political costs. For instance, one of the manifestations of, and one of the reasons for, the crisis of accumulation is that the leading industries—that is, those that were the leading industries in the previous period of growth—tend to lose their positions of leadership, to wallow in particularly serious profitability crises, and to be, if not replaced, displaced to other parts of the world. This was substantially the case in the crisis of the 1870s to 1880s, to which I referred earlier, which was associated with the rise of imperialism. It was also the case of the crisis of the war and interwar years, which resulted in the rise of the United States to economic and political dominance and in the final relative decline of Great Britain, a decline that began after 1870. (Final is perhaps not the right word because there is reason to suspect, and Harold Wilson has felt obliged to deny it to his American hosts, that this time Britain is going to decline still further and practically disappear below the waves—figuratively, of course—I hope only figuratively!)

On the one hand, leading industries such as the automobile industry (which is very evidently in deep trouble the world over) and the textile industry need to develop new technology, while new leading industries based on new technology need to be developed. Such developments, however, can only take place in part through the displacement of previous leading industries. This in turn can only happen if the rate of profit again rises to acceptable levels so as to make it profitable to undertake the massive new investment necessary for the new leading industries. At the same time, industries that have become relatively labor intensive (labor intensive with high-cost labor) are displaced to low-cost labor areas, or replaced by other industries that produce substitute goods through a different sort of technology. One of the obvious areas in which this kind of change is beginning to take place is in the production of new sources of energy to replace petroleum, as well as the revival of old sources of energy. Coal, for example, is again coming into its own, although it is supposed that coal mining will become very different through, for instance, gasification of coal below the ground.

In June 1975 in Europe, Henry Kissinger presented a plan (perhaps a plan is an overstatement, an announcement, at least) for an investment program of $1 trillion to develop new sources of energy, including nuclear, solar, and geothermal. That is a lot of money, almost two-thirds of the entire US gross national product, and before that kind of money will be invested, a few changes will have to take place in the world economy. One of these, about which Kissinger has been particularly adamant, is that the price of petroleum must rise and must remain high in order to make it profitable to develop these alternative sources of energy. If petroleum prices are low, there is no incentive to invest in other sources of energy or to develop the necessary technology.

Another important area, perhaps particularly interesting in Southeast Asia, is the development of the sea (that is to say, both the sea and the seabed) as a source of minerals, and food, particularly protein. This will also require vast new investment and implies far-reaching changes in the international division of labor. The underdeveloped countries, or some of them, have been very worried about this, and at the Law of the Sea conferences in Caracas and Geneva they have sought controls on such development through an international agency with licensing rights. Whether they will achieve this is uncertain. I tend to think it doubtful, and that this development will primarily be in the hands of the major industrial countries, including the Soviet Union, which on this issue sits entirely on the same side of the table as the United States, against the so-called Third World.

Of course, the increase in the price of petroleum has already vastly affected the balance of payments in many countries, not only the consuming countries, but also the producing countries, which have all this new money. This raises questions of investment, and interestingly enough the United States, which has always supported the principle that foreign investment is a great boon to humanity, is now beginning to make all kinds of laws against foreign investment by others in the United States.

Some of the most serious victims of the petroleum price rise have been the nonpetroleum-producing Third World countries, most particularly India, which has had to increase its payments by a vast proportion.

Another area of change in these times of crisis is in the relations between the production of industrial commodities and of raw materials and food products. Here the evidence from the past is not entirely clear, but it would appear that there is a decline (not necessarily absolute but relative) in the importance of industrial commodities (certainly compared to the periods of rapid economic expansion) relative to that of the production of raw materials—though often the increase in the production of raw materials is not across the board for all raw materials and is not necessarily a result of the old technology but of changes in the technology of raw material extraction.

In any event, one of the most important requirements for this process from the point of view of capital is that the rate of profit, which has decreased and may decrease further, must be made to rise again in order to enable the expansion of capital into new areas. And this is likely to involve a whole series of important changes, among them the depression of the wage rate and associated economic, social, and political transformations. There is the important possibility that even though there may be an upturn at the end of the year or at the beginning of 1976, this may be short-lived—and may lead to a further cyclical downturn. This was the pattern in the earlier periods of crisis, but now there are more cyclical downturns, and they are deeper, more frequent, and more coordinated from one part of the world to the other. This is the first time since the end of World War II that in all the major industrial countries there has been an important cyclical downturn. In the United States, for instance, this takes the form of 9 percent unemployment, approximately 8.5 million people unemployed. The prospects are that this unemployment will not be reduced below 7 percent in the next few years. There are at present about 1 million unemployed in each of the major European economies so that altogether in the major industrial countries there are at least 15 million officially unemployed.

This period of crisis, then, like those in the past, may lead to increased internal political conflict and to external international political conflict. It may even, as it has in the past, lead to war.

I would like now to turn to a brief examination of possibilities for different regions of the world, or, more accurately, for different types of countries and different parts of the so-called Third World.

As a result of this period of conflict there is, and there may continue to be, an increase and strengthening in progressive and revolutionary political movements. As an example (though I do not know to what extent this is true), several newspapers have quoted Kissinger as saying that it was Watergate—and Watergate again must be traced to the economic crisis in the world and in the United States—that effectively prevented the United States from politically intervening again against the Vietnamese. This to some extent accounts for the US failure to postpone victory in Vietnam.

Although there is in this period of conflict a partial strengthening and an increase in progressive movements, I think there
is serious reason to fear (or hope, depending on which side you
are on!) that in the long run these may fail unless they follow
the uncompromising example of the Vietnamese.

On the other hand, there is serious reason to suppose that
there will be some of the following kinds of development,
several of which have already begun to take place:

1. In the cheap labor, industrial economies of the Third
World—of the Korea, Taiwan, Singapore, Hong Kong variety
(and important steps are now being made to convert Malaysia
into such an economy)—I think that the needs of capital
worldwide and the needs of capital and the ruling class in these
countries, which have to compete for foreign investment in a
period of crisis, will oblige them to continue to depress the
wage rate and to do so through increased political repression
and even greater increased military intervention and attempts
to establish what might be called some kind of a "military-
corporatist" state.

2. For the cheap labor, raw materials, and food-producing
countries there is also reason to believe that the repression is
likely to increase substantially along the lines of what might be
called the Chilean model. In this brutal repression, over 30,000
people have been killed, hundreds of thousands jailed, and
torture has become institutionalized—all in order to get rid of
the usual democratic institutions and to destroy the labor
movement. In the course of a little more than a year, the real
wage rate has been depressed by approximately 50 percent,
while the economy has been handed to foreign capital on a
silver platter. Foreign capital was begged to invest in raw
materials and in industrial production. Thus far there has been
some investment in raw materials, particularly copper, but
none in industry. There is also an important move to convert
Chile into an agricultural export economy—or return it, since
that was what Chile was before the international grain market
began to decline at the end of the 1920s. The regime wants to
export again, and is in fact doing so, but at the price of starving
the population. This it can only do with political repression, by

imposing a military-fascist state. The military is there; fascism so far less so. Because the regime has been unable to construct a corporatist state, it has had to replace the corporatism by naked brute force and repression.

I think that the Chilean model is by no means limited to Chile. I am not quite sure where to place the Philippines, but it seems to me that it is very clear that the martial law imposed by Marcos is an analogous political instrument for this kind of new integration into world capitalism, or the world market if you prefer, that is in the interest of both world capital and some limited sections of domestic capital. I think that the same thing has begun to happen, and is very likely to continue to happen, in much greater degree in Sri Lanka, in Bangladesh, and in several countries of Latin America, apart from Chile.

3. Another category of Third World country includes Brazil, Mexico, South Africa (if that is to be included in the Third World, which is not clear), and, more doubtfully, Argentina and India. These are economies that went through a stage of import substitution in the 1930s and 1940s, associated with nationalist, relatively progressive, political movements—progressive in that they made the distribution of income more equal, or less unequal, than it had been before. (Insofar as they did so, of course, they were also able to be politically more progressive and less repressive. They did this, it may be suggested, mainly for economic reasons.) Such import substitution meant it was necessary to create an internal market, so that the workers who produced certain kinds of goods, such as textiles, had to have an income in order to buy these same textiles. Therefore there was a wider distribution of income and the emergence of the nationalist-populist regimes associated with Vargas, Peron, Cardenas, and I think the Congress Party in India.

These economies have reached a stage of capital accumulation substantially different from that of most of the Third World. They now have the opportunity to re-enter the international division of labor in a different way, to become relatively much more important exporters, not only of raw materials or of labor-intensive consumer goods of the Singapore variety, but also of capital goods and particularly of automotive and steel products. Brazil, for instance, now exports Volkswagen engines to the United States for the US market—with German capital, of course.

These countries, as I said, once again have an important "opportunity" in a sort of accelerated game of musical chairs in the change in the international division of labor. But the political prospects are now quite dissimilar to those of the 1930s and 1940s, since it is no longer a question of import substitution of consumer goods and an expansion of the internal market. Now the primary area for capital accumulation is capital goods (that consumers do not buy), in the external market, and very importantly in the government, or state, sector, particularly the military; so that there is a vast increase in military procurement and military production in these countries. I think that India's production of the atomic bomb is intimately related to this development.

I suggested that India and Argentina may be a subcategory, inasmuch as it is not clear that they are going to make it. They are facing considerable difficulties: Argentina has been in a permanent state of economic and political crisis for approximately two decades, while the process of economic development in India has drastically slowed down in the last few years and there does not seem to be much prospect of recovery in the foreseeable future—although efforts to that end will be made. These efforts, however, imply a vast increase in political repression, as has been the case with the imposition of emergency rule in India.

4. Then there are another two categories of Third World countries: the first might be called "old intermediate" or "old subimperialist" countries; the other includes the "new subimperialist" ones, of which Iran is perhaps the best example. A number of other petroleum-producing countries are in a position to attempt a similar development to that of Iran. Another case is Venezuela, and perhaps to some extent also Algeria, Nigeria, and Indonesia. In Indonesia, since the coup in 1965, Suharto's regime has made significant efforts to become a sort of Brazil but has so far failed, both economically and politically. However, with its petroleum income it may now be in a

Andre Gunder Frank

better position to attempt that kind of development, including of course the external expansionism—the economic, political, and military dominance of a region, such as Iran is evidently achieving. In the case of Indonesia, as I say, the result is considerably more in doubt.

In the present crisis, there may be some "liberalization" in these subimperialist economies insofar as some that are already subimperialist have the opportunity to move up a productive notch in their participation in the international division of labor, and the same crisis offers the opportunity for some other economies to move into Brazil-type positions. The most obvious case is Iran, but probably a number of other petroleum-producing centers have similar, albeit lesser, opportunities. There is considerable competition in various parts of the world for this kind of position. In the case of the Middle East, for instance, there is competition between Iran, Iraq, Egypt, and Saudi Arabia. It is fairly clear who is going to win: Iran. In some subimperialist centers there may be some degree of liberalization of the political regimes, by comparison to the repression they had before. The ability of some sectors of capital in these economies, in these economic centers, to take advantage of this crisis and move into a different spot in the international division of labor is based on, in part, an opening to foreign capital in the previous period, combined with very severe political repression. In some of these places, but not in India, some "liberalization" of this political repression may now be possible, as seems to have been announced by the Geisel regime in Brazil, and recently in South Africa by Oppenheimer's sudden backing of the "Progressive" Party.

But we will not get a repetition of the kind of populism that we got in the last crisis, because the type of capital accumulation that is necessary for capital in these parts of the world is no longer based on the expansion of the consumer goods industry (textiles) for the internal market, where capital wants the workers who produce the products to consume them also. In this case, capital has to give labor a greater cut in what it produces, so that labor can provide an internal market. The present stage of capital accumulation no longer requires this.

On the contrary, it is not at all suited to the present needs of capital there. Now capital has to produce producers' goods and for the world market. Therefore, we get instead, if I may symbolize, the Indian bomb. The production of the atomic bomb costs a lot of money, but absorbs a lot of capital-producing industry financed by the state. Of course, this is really only a caricature, since not only is the bomb produced, but so are other goods which are not for the domestic consumer.

I would like to add that one important aspect, economically and politically, of this development of subimperialism (as well as of the kind of increasingly repressive outward-oriented development efforts on the part of the first two categories of countries, the Korea-Taiwan model and the Chilean model) is the much increased prospect of war among these under-developed countries; not among all of them, but in the regions in which these economic and political developments forebode increasing threats. I should say not only threats, because we have already had some of these regional wars—for example, the Indo-Pakistan war.

Turning now to social imperialism, as the Chinese call it, in this sort of game of musical chairs with the accelerated change in the international division of labor, before the music stops playing and there is one less chair everybody has to scurry around in order to be able to participate in the international division of labor and not to be left out in the cold, or sitting between two chairs, and that includes the socialist economies. That, I think, is one reason for the Nixon-Brezhnev détente and the vast increase in economic collaboration between the Soviet Union and the Western imperialist countries. Of course, there are also internal reasons, and these are the really important ones. On the one hand, there seem to be economic fluctuations in the socialist economies, with a sort of eight-year cycle in the process of accumulation. They are now in a down phase of that cycle or fluctuation—I am somewhat reluctant to call it a cycle—and in the down phases they are under great pressure to increase their economic contacts with the capitalist world. The fundamental reason for the increased contact is not crop failure, but the inability of the socialist countries to continue satisfactory industrial development without becoming far more integrated into the imperialist economy. What they have to do is to import Western technology. Of course, this "satisfaction" has a class base. It is, in a word, to build the automobile in the Soviet Union, and that for a particular sector of the society. The 1971–1975 five-year plan, for the first time since 1928, calls for more production of consumer goods than of capital goods in the Soviet Union. In the Eastern European countries, the increase in the production of consumer goods relative to capital goods has also increased, but has not yet passed 50 percent. But these are not just any kind of consumer goods. As I say, they are symbolized by the automobile and all that implies about the class structure. With due respect to our colleague in the Soviet Union who says, if I understand him correctly, that there is no more class society in the Soviet Union, all this development says a lot about class structure in the Soviet Union. That is why I prefer to call this the Brezhnev model, rather than the Soviet model. It is not perhaps the Suslov model, for instance.

With this development model, the socialist countries insert themselves into the international division of labor in a way very similar to that of the subimperialist countries. We get a sort of—if one may coin a phrase—social subimperialism of the Soviet Union and a subsocial imperialism of the East European countries. That is to say, they buy technology from the imperialist countries—not first-rank technology, because that is not available to them, but second-rank technology—and use it to produce goods both for the domestic market and for export particularly to the Third World. Despite their payment with raw materials and light manufactures to the imperialist world, the socialist countries are getting an increasingly unfavorable balance of payments with respect to the imperialist countries by their import of this technology. They have to pay for that through export to the Third World, with which they are getting an increasingly favorable balance of payments—thereby, of course, making the balance of payments still more favorable for the Third World as a whole. But they have to pay the imperialist countries with foreign exchange that they earn in the capitalist-dominated periphery. I suggest that this is one reason, though not the entire reason, for Soviet policy with respect to China. China represents a political, ideological, and economic threat of competition to the Soviet Union in certain parts of the Third World, which the Soviet Union attempts to eliminate partly through its ideological battle with China and, of course, through the stationing of a million troops on the Sino-Soviet frontier. In the socialist countries of Eastern Europe, this process is more accelerated and this economic pattern is further advanced, symbolized, shall we say, by Rumania's joining the International Monetary Fund.

Turning now to the imperialist center, we also face a process of South Africanization or the imposition of "1984" policies. Capital is imposing and welcoming the Chilean, Brazilian, and Brezhnev models in the periphery and semiperiphery, there to augment exploitation and superexploitation as well as to revert increasingly to a sort of primitive accumulation—that is, extraction of surplus value with noncapitalist, including "socialist," productive relations but for capitalist accumulation. But insofar as this additional source of surplus value and of profit is still insufficient to stem the tide of the capitalist crisis of accumulation, it will become necessary to increase the rate of exploitation and to reorganize the process of production in the so-called dominant imperialist centers.

A first reaction of capital here is to try to stem the tide through social democracy, through an incomes policy, through getting the Labour Party in England, for instance, to take care of the unions. After the February 1974 elections, for instance, the *Financial Times* of London came out for Wilson instead of Heath, but said very clearly why and what it thought the mandate for Wilson was. According to the *Financial Times,* Wilson did not have anything like a mandate to do what Wedgwood Benn is trying, or supposedly is trying, to do. Labour's main mandate was to cut off the left wing of the Trade Union Congress and to discipline labor. And if it could do that, then it would be fulfilling the job which the *Financial Times* assigns to the Labour government. It is now evident that the Wilson government could not do it—of course, it was evident all along that they would never be able to. In other parts of the imperialist world, capital is also attempting, as a first line of defense, to reorganize the economy and the society through social democracy. My suspicion is that this is increasingly going to fail. Even in the citadel of social democracy, in Scandinavia, it has rather fizzled. Everybody is governing on a razor's edge, either with a 50-50 government or a minority government. In the last elections around the capitalist world, we saw an increase in minority governments, none of which is going to have a sufficient political base to face the deepening economic crisis, which became considerably deeper in 1974. These governments are not going to be able to handle this crisis.

My suspicion is that the next order of the day is governments of "national unity," as a political attempt to handle the economic crisis. And these governments of national unity, I think, will be designed to pave the way for 1984. In some places, perhaps, it will be impossible to establish a government of national unity and there may simply be a military takeover straight away, which will impose 1984 without going through a long drawn-out process. In Britain, even the press already discusses this prospect. That is to say, the class struggle, around the issue of the reorganization of the economy and the society, becomes ever more acute in the face of this economic crisis. As I mentioned earlier, one of the major ways to try to overcome this crisis is to introduce new technology, but only when the time is ripe, when the economy has been reorganized, and the profit rate has risen again, if it does. Then we will get new technology, particularly in the energy sector—nuclear fusion or solar energy, which may become profitable through the increase in the price of petroleum, and the mining of the sea— hence the Caracas Conference; developments in biochemistry and perhaps in genetics will feed into the 1984 that is on the horizon.

Therefore, the class struggle is going to turn on the attempt of capital not only to depress the wage rate, but also to reorganize the economy internationally, interregionally, and intersectorally—for instance, through worker participation and through the Volvo model of eliminating the assembly line and establishing small work groups. This becomes possible and desirable, particularly in countries which no longer mass-produce standardized products but instead move into a high-technology (such as aerospace production of relatively few capital goods that are highly capital intensive), produce labor-intensive goods in cheap-labor countries, and move the auto-mobile and steel industries to Brazil and the Soviet Union. This happens not only for economic reasons, but also for political ones. The most politically sensitive mass-production industries are moved out and in this way capital can control labor in the imperialist countries, while it can produce in the Soviet Union not only at a low wage but also with disciplined labor and no strikes. Thus capital can use this move as a ploy in bargaining and disciplining labor in the imperialist countries. This raises the question, for instance, whether in the pursuit of the class struggle, labor should go along with this kind of reorganization of the work process and with the implementa-tion of worker participation, which I suspect in the long run is really helping capital to do what it has to do in order to reorganize the economy.

In sum, capitalism may or may not be on its last legs. The present crisis of accumulation obliges capital to reorganize the economy, society, and "polity" (I really do not know the difference among all these), through a qualitative change in the division of labor and the imposition of new technology, which capital can only do if it becomes profitable to do so and if labor is sufficiently disciplined and reorganized to permit it. The question of whether capitalism does survive this crisis through reorganization and can thus go on to another major upswing, such as that after 1896 and after 1945, lies in the outcome of the class struggle, on whether the policy of the working class prohibits or permits, let alone facilitates, the reorganization of the economy in the interest and needs of capital. Agnelli, the head of Fiat in Italy, says that he now finds that the policy of the Communist Party of Italy is much better, much more rational, than that of Fanfani and the Christian Democratic Party. If Agnelli thinks that, it is because the political policy of the Communist Party of Italy is designed to collaborate with the reorganization of the economy and society in the interests of capital, and to permit not only the technological revolution but also the depression of the wage rate. These measures are necessary to get capital out of the doldrums and into a new phase of expansion after 1984—"after 1984" in the sense of the imposition of 1984 in order to reorganize the society.

The question here is the kind of class alliances the working class makes. The *compromesso historico* of the Italian Communist Party to join the government in alliance with the Christian Democrats symbolizes a working-class collaborationist political program designed by the major Communist parties in and outside of Western Europe. In Chile, for instance, the policy of the Communist Party before Allende, during Allende, and now again after Allende, has been to make an alliance with the Christian Democrats. The reaction to developments in Chile by Marchais, the secretary general of the French Communist Party, was, "Well, Allende really didn't have a base to do anything since he didn't have 51 percent of the vote." And then came Berlinguer, the secretary general of the Italian Communist Party, who said, "Well, it's not only that Allende didn't have 51 percent of the vote; you have to have more than 51 percent of the vote. You have to have 51 percent of the vote *and* the Christian Democrats in order to do anything." If that is the political line of the working class in the coming or current crisis, then it seems to me that there is absolutely no doubt that we are paving the shortest road to 1984. There is a very close connection between the political organization and the political line of the working-class movement in general and the Communist parties in particular. In order to stem the tide of 1984, we need a political line and a political organization that is radically different from the one we now have in the major imperialist countries, including most particularly Japan. The electoral policy of the Japanese Communist Party has probably helped to push the country the farthest down the road to the imposition of a sort of 1984. However hard it is to define and however difficult to construct, that is why we so urgently need an alternative revolutionary political policy and organization which can lead us not to 1984 but to Hasta La Victoria Siempre!

4. WORLD CRISIS AND UNDERDEVELOPMENT

The last coup d'état in the Third World took place on October 6, 1976, in Thailand and has resulted in considerable repression, not only of ordinary democratic liberties but of the people. Strikes have been banned, and the junta says that it does not expect to allow elections again for sixteen years, while implementing, in four-year stages, a whole program of social reorganization. Commenting on this coup, the French newspaper *Le Monde* of October 20, 1976, made a survey of Southeast Asia since the victory in Vietnam, Laos, and Cambodia (Kampuchea) in 1975. *Le Monde* observed that despite, and perhaps to some extent because of, this popular victory in Indochina, repression has been increasing in the remainder of the countries of the region. In Indonesia, there has been repression since the Suharto coup in 1965. In the Philippines, repression has increased, there has been martial law for over two years, strikes are banned, etc. In Singapore, repression has increased recently, as manifested particularly in the universities. In Malaysia, repression has also increased: in a letter to the editor of the *Far Eastern Economic Review* on October 22, 1976, the opposition leader in the parliament complained about the new labor laws that are designed to permit greater exploitation, he says, of Malaysian labor and to exempt particular firms from compliance with the labor laws in order to be able, he says, to attract foreign investment on more favorable

This is a revised version of a lecture that was delivered at the Catholic University of Tilberg, the Netherlands, in October 1976 and published in *Contemporary Crises* 1: 243–260, 1977. It is reprinted by permission of the publisher.

terms. There has been increasing repression, particularly of labor, in Korea and Taiwan.

In India, according to several sources, particularly since Gandhi's imposition of emergency rule on June 26, 1975, 175,000 people have been detained. The socialist labor leader Fernandes is now being tried, but the press is unanimous in observing that the number of days lost through strikes has declined and that, although there have been lockouts and layoffs, labor discipline has increased. This has been welcomed by foreign capital, which in turn has received increasingly favorable terms from the government. There have been similar tendencies in Bangladesh, where there is also in essence a military government. There is also increasing repression in Sri Lanka and so forth.

In the Middle East, the momentary defeat of the Palestinians and of the progressive forces in Lebanon has meant a significant move to the right. This defeat has occurred particularly through the intervention of Syria, which, after the installation of the Assad government, moved considerably to the right but not enough, at least until recently, to intervene militarily against the left and the Palestinians in Lebanon. As we know, in Egypt government policy has been to break with the Soviet Union and to open the door diplomatically, politically, and economically to Western imperialism and foreign capital, and—very significantly—to shift the balance of power to the right. Even Algeria has not offered any significant support to the Palestinians in this last half year. It is not necessary to mention the very right-wing regimes of Saudi Arabia and others, which were always there. Summing up, we can say that there has been a significant shift to the right, economically and politically, nationally and internationally, and that the Palestinians have been the most visible, but not the only, victims of this shift.

Latin America, as my son observed in a conversation with me, is "almost all in the hands of the soldiers" (his expression for military regimes). There are only two countries—Colombia and Venezuela—that are not now under military regimes. These are not just any kind of military regime, but regimes that, beginning with Brazil and now including Chile, are

following a particularly repressive political policy and instituting an economic policy associated with the name of Milton
Friedman. (Friedman has just won the Nobel Prize, perhaps in
part for the advice he gave to the Chilean junta, which is
implementing his economic policy.) But this policy is not
limited to the Chilean junta. It is now being implemented in
Argentina and Uruguay. In Peru, there was a significant shift to
the right during the summer with the elimination of the so-
called left-wing elements in the military junta. (There is widespread agreement that this was done in part through blackmail
by US banks.) This was denounced even by the *New York
Times* (see the *International Herald Tribune* for August 5 and
September 3, 1976). When the Peruvian regime was in serious
balance-of-payment difficulties and asked for credits, it was
told that it would have to eliminate its left wing and change its
internal economic policy in order to get these credits. Even
Mexico devalued its currency about six weeks ago, while still
under the outgoing government of President Echeverria—a
devaluation that means a decline in the standard of living of the
masses of the population.

In this disturbing panorama of the Third World, Africa
seems to be an exception by virtue of the revolution in Ethiopia,
the victory of the MPLA in Angola, and in general the liberation of the ex-Portuguese colonies, Mozambique, Angola, and
Guinea-Bissau. The situation in the southern part of Africa
adds to the optimism: the Smith regime in Rhodesia is virtually
certain of being toppled and the Vorster regime in South
Africa, though not in danger of disappearing, is having its
difficulties. I am not quite so optimistic on the basis of these
successes as some may be. In the case of Ethiopia, there has
already been a significant shift back to the right, and what the
final consequences of events in the southern part of Africa will
be we do not know. We can see that Kissinger, Callaghan, and
others are making serious efforts to save the situation, from
their point of view, and they may succeed.

Southern Europe might perhaps be regarded as another
exception, in that there is an increase in popular and labor
mobilization in Portugal—although I would say that the Portu-

guese revolution has already been defeated, at least in this particular round. There has been a liberalization in Spain, increased influence for the Communist Party in Italy, the possibility of an electoral victory of Mitterand in France, etc. Again, what is promised by such events is hard to know. I had the feeling in Spain of euphoria which reminded me of Chile during the Allende years, but which seems to me to be not quite realistic, given the objective circumstances inside Spain, in Europe, and in the world as a whole.

In Northern Europe, in North America, and in Japan there is more or less unanimous agreement that a political shift to the right is manifesting itself through elections: for instance, the recent defeat (after forty years) of social democracy in Sweden and the marginal electoral shift to the right in the recent German election. Public opinion surveys indicate a similar shift in the United States. More important, perhaps, is what lies behind these—I hate to say superficial, tip-of-the-iceberg— political manifestations. On July 19, 1976, *U.S. News & World Report,* one of the three major US news weeklies, said, "Experts expect business to climb for years to come." They then interviewed a number of people to the effect that business is expanding and will continue to do so. They even quoted Lawrence Klein, who is principal economic adviser to Jimmy Carter and head of one of the three major econometric business forecasting services in the United States. Klein said that with proper government policies this policy of expansion and recovery pursued since mid-1975 could lead to a replay of the 1960s boom. The funny thing is that if you read not only the opening prediction but the analysis of the situation, you get a very different picture. Furthermore, since then the recovery has faltered, and there have been two or three months of reduced rates of growth and renewed increases in the rate of unemployment. That may or may not be responsible for the survey in the latest issue of *U.S. News & World Report* (October 25, 1976), which said the opposite of what had been said in July. Now the magazine surveyed what it called "business economists"—that is to say, economists who work for big businesses such as banks and major corporations—and asked questions like how long the recovery is likely to last and when a renewed recession could be expected. Over half—54 percent—of these business economists said that they expected a renewed recession in 1978, 25 percent said 1979, and 6 percent said 1977. Indeed, there is already discussion of whether the renewed downturn in the growth rate and the renewed upturn in unemployment in the United States, which began last spring and has continued into the fall months, is simply a momentary jiggle in the curve of expansion or whether it signifies that the expansion, the recovery, is already finished. One of the things that Klein observed is that the post-1975 recovery has been almost exclusively based on consumer demand and the need to replenish inventory; it has not been based on productive investment anywhere—not in Japan, the United States, Germany, or any of the major industrialized countries. This has also been remarked upon by such politicians as Jacques Chirac before, and I think also after, he resigned as prime minister of France. It seems to me that this is perhaps the most highly significant of these observations, because without an increase in productive investment the prospects for the maintenance of the recovery are very dim. I agree with those of the business economists quoted in *U.S. News & World Report* who expect a renewed recession in 1978 or even earlier. I also agree with those who said that the 1978 recession is likely to be deeper than the one that we just went through in 1974–1975, which was the deepest, the most coordinated in the sense of being simultaneous in all the major industrialized countries, recession since the depression of the 1930s.

Another item in this regard: the Organization of Economic Cooperation and Development (OECD), a collective economic body of the industrialized countries from North America, Europe, and Japan which has headquarters in Paris, issues the *Economic Outlook* twice a year, in December and July, which reviews the major economic developments of the past and tries to preview the prospects for the immediate future. In the December 1975 issue, the magazine talked about a moderate recovery and a moderation in the recovery, which it said governments of the industrialized countries welcomed, because it was hoped that the moderation in the recovery, including relatively restrictive monetary and fiscal policies, would avoid the renewed take-off of inflation. In a special supplement of July 1976, on "growth scenario to 1980," which the OECD takes great care to qualify as a "realistic prospect" not a prediction or goal, the OECD announced "a deceleration of the growth trend, compared to the previous decade, to 4 percent a year beginning in 1973." This "is intended to indicate the difficulties and problems against which all economic policy is likely to come up in the course of these years." Then, specifically to encourage and render new capital investment policy, the OECD scenario envisages the necessity of "important modifications of the internal distribution of income, from the earnings of labor to the earnings of capital." According to *Le Monde* (July 29, 1976), political decisions of this sort can already be seen in operation, particularly in Britain, Italy, France, and Portugal, all of which have announced austerity measures. In Britain, the action has supposedly been taken in response to the balance of payments crisis and the decline of the pound. Milton Friedman, the Nobel Prize winner, says that the British government is spending too much and has to cut down its expenditures in order to end the slipping of the pound and of the British economy in general. The Andreotti government in Italy, with the support of the Communist Party, is also imposing drastic austerity measures. Raymond Barre, a professional economist who just became prime minister of France, has also tried to impose an austerity program, although so far it is meeting with considerable resistance: as you may recall, about ten days ago there was a one-day nationwide general strike in opposition to Barre's plan. According to the estimates in *Le Monde,* the plan would take between 5 and 15 percent of the income away from particular income groups in France. If that is the case, then it is easy to see why there should be resistance not only expressed through a general strike, but also through other political mechanisms. And finally, in Portugal, the Soares government is engaged in undoing the reforms that had occurred since the so-called revolution of April 25, 1974, by imposing a very servere austerity program.

Elsewhere, where such austerity programs are not yet being imposed because the economies are not in such serious difficulties, there is nonetheless evidence of political and fiscal attempts to cut back on financial assistance, education, health, and similar services.

These are some of the manifestations of the present crisis. But what is behind these manifestations and how does it relate to the underdeveloped countries? It seems to me that world capitalism is going through, or has entered into, another general crisis of accumulation, analogous to that of the period between 1914 and 1945, which includes the two wars and the depression and which produced the rise of fascism as a direct political and economic response to that crisis. The adjustments that were achieved through fascism in Germany, Italy, and Japan, and the related destruction of the labor unions, the depression of the wage rate, the defeat of Germany in World War II and the victory of the United States, which made it the dominant power in the world, were essential to the postwar recovery of world capitalism. The long postwar boom lasted until the middle of the 1960s, when it seemed to falter and the rate of profit in the major industrialized countries began to decline again. There was a recession in several countries in 1967, the temporarily successful attempt to stave off the recession in the United States through the expenditures connected with the war against Vietnam finally gave way to the 1970 recession. In 1971 there was the currency crisis, the devaluation of the dollar, and the elimination of the payment of gold against the dollar. Then in 1973 there was the petroleum crisis, and the 1973–1975 recession, which was blamed on the sheikhs, although it had actually begun several months before that. By mid-1974 it was no longer possible to blame the Arabs for the recession, and Kissinger, Wilson, and Schmidt began to admit a bit more realistically that there was in fact a serious economic recession—an investment crisis. So they began to talk in terms of 1929–1930 and the danger of a great depression.

The 1973–1975 recession was, in fact, the most serious that the capitalist world had known since 1930. Official unemployment, which is of course always less than real unemployment, rose to over 17 million in the industrialized countries. Although it has in some places again declined, it has not been eliminated anywhere and in some places has continued to increase, particularly in Great Britain. In the United States, the maximum unemployment rate of 9.2 percent was reached in May 1975; it then declined to about 7 percent, but has recently begun to inch up again, and is now 7.8 percent. Remember that these are all *official rates* and *national averages,* which means that in many major cities unemployment is still more than the 10 percent official figure, and in many sectors unemployment remains very much higher (20 percent for white youth and 40 percent for nonwhite youth). To add to the gloomy picture, there is nearly universal agreement that there are no prospects for eliminating this unemployment in the foreseeable future. On the contrary, if we face a renewed recession in a year or so, possibly less, unemployment will necessarily rise again, but this time beginning from an already high level. At the same time, continued inflation means that orthodox or bourgeois economic theory and policy cannot offer a solution, since neither contemplates the possibility of simultaneous unemployment and inflation. In this regard I can offer a theory of inflation which may be simplistic but which I think is more realistic than the cost-push and demand-pull arguments that we usually hear. That theory, which is also supported by the evidence and even by some business statements, is simply that when profits decline, or threaten to decline, businesses raise prices in order to defend their rates of profit: and that is why we have inflation. That can be demonstrated to some degree: (1) in the countries in which the rate of profit has declined the most, the rate of inflation is the highest, and (2) in the industries that are the most monopolized, and the ability to set prices the greatest, price rises have been the highest, while in the most competitive industries they have been the lowest.

We are living in, or entering into, another major world crisis of capital accumulation in which the rate of profit has declined and in which profitable investment opportunities are smaller, or no longer exist, particularly in the sectors and geographical areas in which there had previously been expansion by leading industries. In order to repeat a long boom, such as that of the postwar period, many transformations and developments are necessary. First, the rate of profit has to increase again. Second, capital needs the development of new technology—in Schumpeterian terminology, innovation, not simply invention—in major areas, such as energy, the seas, and so forth. Kissinger has proposed an investment program in new sources of energy that would cost $1 trillion. But before this can take place, the conditions of profitability have to change: old industries have to be replaced by new ones and existing labor processes have to be changed. The international division of labor has to be significantly modified. In the crisis of the 1870s and 1880s, the rise of classical imperialism was one of the major manifestations of this necessary change in the international division of labor. Now, as then, the underdeveloped countries—the misnamed Third World—will of course play a very significant role.

I have already reviewed some of the political manifestations of this new participation in the international division of labor, but I must still examine what lies behind them. First of all, there is an increasing differentiation both *among* and *within* countries of the so-called Third World. The intermediate economies and regimes—also called subimperialist economies or powers—are able to take advantage of this crisis in order to find a new place in the international division of labor. They become producers and exporters of capital goods and machinery, as when Brazil exports Volkswagen engines to the United States. Some new centers can aspire to an analogous subimperialist role. This is particularly the case for Iran, which is using its petroleum earnings in a significant attempt at industrialization. However, these subimperialist economies have also been faltering. The Brazilian miracle ended in 1974, and since the petroleum crisis Brazil has had serious balance of payments problems. Even Iran, despite the massive amounts of foreign exchange that it has received from petroleum, has begun to borrow again and has cut back on its ambitious investment program. South Africa, another of the major subimperialist powers, is in significant economic difficulties in part because of the decline in the price of gold, while such potentially subimperialist powers as Argentina and India have already clearly failed, and by virtue of their failure have had to impose regimes that will come to terms with this failure—as we see in the so-called state of emergency in India and the new military government in Argentina. Then there are lesser powers: also based primarily on petroleum, they can and do aspire to some kind of intermediate role in the international division of labor. For instance, Venezuela, Nigeria, and Indonesia display hopes that already appear essentially frustrated and will probably continue to be so.

Another development is the transfer of labor, the resettlement of labor-intensive industries from the industrialized central economies to some of the underdeveloped countries; Korea, Taiwan, Hong Kong, and Singapore were the first major examples. The transferred industries have included textile manufacturing, electronic components production, and so on. This practice has spread to other countries: Malaysia, the Philippines, Tunisia, Morocco, even Haiti. There, instead of import substitution, you now have a policy of what might be called export substitution, or export promotion of so-called nontraditional industrial or manufacturing exports. Some underdeveloped countries aspire to do the same thing, but cannot compete and must be content to continue to produce raw materials for the world market. In still other countries— particularly Chile—there is a conscious deindustrialization taking place. With the application of Friedman's shock treatment in the middle of 1975, industrial production has gone down 25 percent (according to the Chilean Association of Manufacturers). It would have declined even more if it had not been for the relative success of exporting a significant and increasingly large proportion of domestic industrial production to the so-called world market. But the Chilean military regime has not been successful in attracting new investment into manufacturing for export and instead finds itself obliged to rely on the expansion of mineral and agricultural raw material exports. There are quite a number of other countries that fall into this category, and the World Bank, which used to finance only infrastructure for certain kinds of industrial development by the multinationals in the underdeveloped countries, has markedly shifted its investment program to support more agricultural production and agricultural production for export.

What is significant in this development from the political standpoint is that when there was a policy of import substitution, it was necessary to maintain or expand the internal market for these commodities, and to do this it was necessary to have an income distribution policy that would enable the working class to purchase at least a portion of the commodities they produced. This necessity provided an economic basis for a relatively more equal distribution of income. It made possible an alliance between the bourgeoisie and the working class in a variety of populist regimes. The situation in the present world crisis, in which there is a transfer of industrial production from center to periphery, is not only different, but—to exaggerate a bit—is precisely the opposite. Since industrial production is now increasingly for export, and raw material production remains for export, the producers are no longer the consumers of the products they produce. Therefore, it is not in the interests of capital that the working class in these countries have an income sufficiently great to provide a local effective demand for these products; on the contrary, from the point of view of capital the producers are only that, and are not consumers. They are a cost, a wage cost, and it is in the interest of capital that this be as low as possible. If producers cannot purchase commodities out of their wages, it does not matter because they are not to be sold in the national market anyway. Export promotion thus removes the economic basis for an alliance between local capital, the working class, and the unions in these countries, and there is economic pressure to reduce the wage rate as much as possible. There is competition by these countries—by local capital, which associates itself with the process as well as among governments—to receive as large a share of the production as possible, or to maximize its participation in the international division of labor by reducing the cost of production to the minimum. This in turn means reducing the wages of labor in order to attract production. This is what the opposition leader of the Malaysian parliament, to whom I referred earlier, meant when he denounced the recent revision of the labor laws and the exemption of certain firms from compliance with them. First of all you make the labor laws more favorable to capital in general, and then, he says, you exempt certain firms from compliance. This is partciularly the case in the so-called free trade or export promotion zones, where the government sets up a sort of enclave in which it provides cheap labor and public utilities—electricity, water, and transportation. No customs duties are charged for the importation of raw materials and components, and their processing and reshipment outward to the world market takes place within these zones in which all strikes are forbidden and labor is totally repressed.

This is a necessary component of the new development in the international division of labor and implies the necessity to repress the working class and the peasantry. It also implies the necessity of increasing collaboration between the state and international capital through the development of a state capitalism that will collaborate with international capital, with the multinationals. This in turn implies the need to rely on corporative forms, and particularly military corporative forms, of social organization. That is why it is no accident that practically every country in Latin America is now in the hands of the soldiers. Moreover, these are not military regimes of the 1930s or the nineteenth century, where some general sets himself up and makes a banana republic deal with the British or US imperialists. They are regimes built upon *institutionalized collaboration* between local capital, the military state, the multinationals, and, of course, the governments to which the multinationals align themselves. There are two more things I should underline in this regard. One is that as part of this economically determined development of the military corporatist state, it is necessary to develop a new ideology to legitimize the repression. That new ideology can be summarized in the words "national security," which is the flag that is being waved by a number of these regimes. National security, as it is now used, no longer means simply military defense against some real or threatened invasion from a neighboring country: it means economic development and the security of economic, political, and social arrangements. The other aspect that should perhaps be underlined in this regard is the likelihood—I would say certainty—of increasing wars between many of these under-developed countries in the Third World. These are particularly likely under the stewardship of the subimperialist powers which have been arming themselves to the teeth.

To conclude, these political manifestations are only the first repercussions of a world capitalist economic crisis. The under-developed countries are destined to play new roles in this crisis through the international division of labor, and the crisis is bound to involve them in the first instance through their balance of payments difficulties and their terrible debt problems. The inability to pay off their debts has led to the need to go to the International Monetary Fund, the Club of Paris, and the banks in the industrialized countries to ask for assistance, which, if rendered, then imposes obligations that necessitate severe austerity measures—often going considerably beyond those that have so far been imposed in countries such as Britain and Italy.

The underdeveloped countries have to do their share in helping international capital recover its profitability and launch a major new wave of investment in order to produce certain commodities in the Third World. This will, in turn, make it possible for the industrialized countries to go on to a so-called new technological revolution and produce the more sophisticated products in the "developed" countries. In other words, capital needs to take the investment out of textiles and automobiles and put it into new technology. We have to ask ourselves to what extent is the Third World's contribution to the emerging new international division of labor—or if you wish, the new international economic order—sufficient to overcome the crisis of capital accumulation? And to what extent, if it is not sufficient (as I think it is not), is it necessary for very far-reaching economic, political, and social changes to take place in the industrialized countries themselves? What we now see in Britain and Italy are only the very first steps of the imposition of austerity measures, through recourse to social democratic parties such as the Labour Party, which is supposed to be able to discipline the labor unions, or recourse to the cooperation tactics of the Communist Party of Italy in getting labor to accept the austerity measures that capital requires. This may be insufficient to stem the tide of the crisis. To what extent may other political forms then be necessary for capital? To what extent will capital also have to find a new ideology to replace that of the "American way of life" and "growth" that has been dominant in the postwar world, but is no longer sufficiently convincing when we see unemployment and inflation increasing and no prospects of eliminating them? No policies seem to work and certainly most theories are unable to explain why not. Thus there is in both the industrialized and the underdeveloped countries the beginning of a serious ideological crisis, in which capital will have to find an alternative ideology to legitimize its rule and the various drastic austerity measures that it will try to impose on labor.

5. IMPERIALISM, CRISIS, AND SUPEREXPLOITATION IN THE THIRD WORLD

An economic crisis, a crisis of capital accumulation on a world level like the one we are experiencing today, requires the restructuring of the world economy. This kind of restructuring is not limited to the economy but also extends to social, political, and ideological structures at the world and national levels. Restructuring is underway in Europe—for example, between the northern European countries (especially Germany) and southern Europe. England, which increasingly resembles southern Europe, is a possible exception because from being the hegemonic power it declined relatively during the 1873–1895 crisis and lost its world position absolutely during the last crisis, from 1913 to World War II. In the current economic crisis, it appears that Great Britain will cease to be a "great power," and that the United Kingdom will probably cease to be united, as Scotland and later probably Wales secede.

Thus a differentiation process is occurring within Europe itself, and it implies the substitution of new industries for those that were the leading ones up until now: for instance, through the development of new energy sources. This is what Kissinger had in mind when he proposed an expensive plan to create new energy sources; for such a large investment to be profitable, the rate of profit, which has been falling since the mid-1960s, would have to go up again.

One of the mechanisms for achieving that is the application of austerity measures of precisely the kind that are currently

This essay is based on a lecture that was delivered in Spanish at the University of Barcelona in May 1977. It was translated by Mimi Keck.

being put into effect in many European countries—Portugal, Finland, Sweden, Denmark, England, France (where a professional economist is in charge of the Barre plan), and Italy, where the austerity plan is being imposed with the PCI decidedly and openly supporting the Andreotti government, not only in general, but on the plan itself. The Eurocommunists are being called upon to help the bourgeoisie impose these measures and say that they are dedicated to doing so. I suggest that even in Spain there will be an austerity plan after the elections (of June 15, 1977)—in fact, the elections will probably be a major instrument for finding a political solution that will allow an austerity plan to be imposed in Spain as well.

What will happen after the imposition of austerity plans remains to be seen. I am sure that they are doomed to failure, since they are not capable of solving the problems posed by the economic crisis at the world or national level, either for the bourgeoisie or for the working class. Beyond the attempt to impose austerity plans through the mediation of social democratic types of parties or governments, it will probably be a matter of imposing even more austere policies through governments of so-called national unity or national salvation. In a certain sense, there are already the beginnings of such a government in Italy, where the Communist Party, after the "historic compromise," supports and maintains a Christian Democratic government and its austerity plan (as it did in the postwar years).

A bit of historical perspective is needed here. We know that in the past economic crises have been the occasion for profound change. For example, as Paul Sweezy and Harry Magdoff have noted, the 1873 crisis was the antechamber for imperialism; I would go even further and say that the crisis was the immediate cause of imperialism which, in turn, was the form capitalism discovered in order to get out of the accumulation crisis it was undergoing and which resulted in imperialism on the one hand and in monopoly capitalism on the other. That is to say, during that crisis a major qualitative change was already taking place in the international and intersectoral divisions of labor. Another such change occurred during the great crisis of this century, in the 1930s and 1940s: it was this that was fundamentally responsible for sharpening the class struggle in a way that led to popular fronts in some countries and fascist regimes in others—either because of the emergence of popular front governments, or because popular mobilizations began to go beyond limits tolerable to the bourgeoisie. All this only shows that certain kinds of political events are produced during times of economic crisis, impelled by the problems that the crisis generates in the political arena. But at the root of these political changes is the need for a modification of the international division of labor, like the one that is in process today.

Although I will principally be discussing the so-called Third World, I initially referred to the metropolitan part of the imperialist world. I believe that it is indispensible to understand what is happening in one part in order to understand what is going on in the other. In effect, the world economic crisis is affecting the international division of labor, not only among the developed countries but also among the underdeveloped countries. A rapid qualitative differentiation is taking place in the underdeveloped world, the Third World. The press already calls the extremes of this process the fourth world, fifth world, and so forth.

For example, the Third World countries, which underwent a certain kind of industrial development based on what has been called import substitution, resulting from the previous crisis and postwar development, have become, to a certain extent, economies that could be classified as intermediate, or semiperipheral. After the Brazilian experience, these began to be called subimperialist. These countries already participate in the international division of labor in a different way, exporting not so much raw materials or simple manufactured goods but industrial goods coming from heavy industry, engineering, and—significantly—from the armaments industry. This is true for Brazil, where for a long time capital accumulation has not been based on simple consumer goods, but rather on the sector which produces the means of production (Sector I, in Marxist terms), and which already participates in the export of such products to other parts of the world. Up to a point, this also applies to Mexico.

There are other more or less industrialized intermediate economies which have tried to become part of the international division of labor by following the Brazilian model. Argentina is an example, but there it has not yet been possible to impose this model because the bourgeoisie has not been able to break the power of the workers' movement. Consequently, producing for the world market has been neither profitable nor competitive. This is also true for India, which has a developed heavy industry sector, but which has not been able to imitate the Brazilian model. And, with other particularities, the same is true for South Africa and in a certain sense Israel.

One aspect of these intermediate and subimperialist economies that I would like to emphasize is their growing specialization in arms production. I am not talking about submachine guns and pistols, but heavier and more modern armaments: fighter planes, rockets, and advanced electronic components. It is worth mentioning that Spain also stands out in this respect. And we are talking about production destined for export, not merely for the domestic market. In the case of Israel, approximately half of all industrial exports are military equipment.

There is another set of economies that aspire to an intermediate and subimperialist position. Iran intends to develop industry with the income from oil exports. This will not be import substitution, but export production of petrochemicals and steel, the latter based on the most modern techniques, using gas furnaces (employing local gas, a method which has only come into use recently). There are other underdeveloped economies which, like Iran, aspire to a subintermediate level in the international division of labor by investing the foreign exchange earned from oil exports; they include some OPEC countries—Venezuela, Indonesia, Nigeria, Algeria. This industrialization is also oriented toward the world market, not only for the internal market.

Another group of underdeveloped economies, which has been growing rapidly since the beginning of the 1970s, has won its place in the international division of labor by specializing in the production of manufactured goods for the world market based on cheap labor. This process began in the early 1960s in

South Korea and later in Taiwan. The initial impetus was undoubtedly political, given the strategic importance of both countries. In the border area, between Mexico and the United States, assembly plants were also set up, followed by other kinds of production; this took advantage of Mexico's cheap labor to produce goods destined for the American and world markets. Later on, this form of specialization was developed in Hong Kong and Singapore and is now expanding to Malaysia and the Philippines. Free zones are being established—not free trade zones, which have been familiar for centuries, but rather production zones where the multinationals provide the raw materials and industrial components, which are assembled and then reexported. This has been done in South Korea, Taiwan, and Malaysia, and is now spreading to Haiti, El Salvador, Tunisia, Morocco, and many other countries. I recently saw a list of fifty-five countries where textiles, electronics, and other labor-intensive commodities are produced for the world market.

To continue the review of the different ways in which Third World countries are inserted into the world market, it is enough to cite that group of economies whose principal form of insertion is through the export of raw materials, minerals, or agricultural products. There has been a boom in production for export in these economies, but it is taking a different form today from the forms that predominated during the postwar period. In particular, "agribusiness" multinationals are going into various countries in the Third World to produce agricultural products, both food and industrial, for export to the world market. Countries like Chile, which had reached a certain level of industrialization based on import substitution, are now deindustrializing. A policy analogous to the Chilean one is being put into practice in Argentina as well. In other words, they are passing over forty years of import substitution to return to an economic and political model that dates back to the years prior to the crisis of the 1930s, when Argentina's economy was based on two raw material exports, livestock and wheat. But two phenomena seem to be superimposed in Argentina: first, participation in the increase of exports to the world market, and second, an attempt to discipline the working class by bringing industry to such a standstill that their political power is broken. Once this has been accomplished— if it is accomplished—then Argentina may also be able to take a place in the international division of labor as an exporter of manufactured goods. It cannot do this now because its labor force is too highly paid and because no company would invest in Argentina, or in Chile, to export manufactured goods under present conditions.

One last category of underdeveloped economy that I would like to mention includes those sectors that seem to play virtually no role in the international division of labor. The example most often given is Bangladesh, though it applies just as well to large areas of India, and parts of other intermediate sub-imperialist countries, like the Brazilian northeast. These areas are being asked to accept a "lifeboat" policy: if the lifeboat is full and more people try to get into it, everyone will drown, so it is better that some drown in order that others may survive. This argument is used to justify a policy of abandoning those people who cannot play any role in the international division of labor: let them go under, literally, through disease, war, famine, and so forth. It is no accident that disease is spreading again in large areas of South Asia. In India, for example, malaria, which had been controlled after two decades of effort following World War II, is rampant again: there seems to be an intentional policy to let these people go under.

I have tried to outline briefly the differentiation process taking place in the so-called Third World. I would now like to point out the common themes that transcend this differentiation process.

Beyond imposing austerity policies in Western capitalist countries to bring the rate of profit, and later the investment rate, up again, capital is calling upon the underdeveloped countries to collaborate to the same end by contributing more surplus value through greater exploitation, and, especially, through superexploitation. Economically, this demand translates into a balance of payments crisis, an increase in austerity measures and exploitation, and the suppression of those domestic policies designed to confront these crises. Politically, the accumulation crisis leads to a sharpening of the class and national liberation struggles. In some parts of the Third World the latter has met with a great deal of success, as in Indochina, or (relatively) in Angola and Mozambique, and, more doubtfully, in Ethiopia. But up to now, these are more the exception than the rule. The rule in the Third World, for the moment, is a turn toward the reactionary and repressive right. I would say that aside from the sharpening of the class struggle, the most important reason for this is the world economic crisis and the changes in the international division of labor, which I referred to previously. Seen from a Third World perspective, this change at the international level and this process of differentiation appears as a campaign for promotion and intensification of exports of the following type: means of production (capital goods) from the intermediate, subimperialist economies; manufactured goods from South Korea, Taiwan, Hong Kong, Malaysia, and elsewhere; and agricultural and mineral products from other countries.

Export promotion is justified by the claim that there is a balance of payments crisis which must be dealt with by increasing exports. But it is also justified by an argument that such production leads to industrialization and an increase in technical capacity.

There is clearly a balance of payments crisis, most notably in precisely those underdeveloped countries that have been most actively promoting exports, like Brazil (which today has a foreign debt of $30 billion), South Korea, and Mexico. This policy, then, does not in any way resolve balance of payments problems—rather the opposite. Specialization in the production and export of manufactured goods requires an ever greater increase in the import of the components, raw materials, and technology needed to make the product.

This policy is clearly different from earlier import-substitution policies, even though in this case the result is the substitution of one import for another (that is to say, the import of textiles is replaced by the import of the machinery to produce them). Those textiles, however, were to be sold on the domestic

market, which required a certain level of effective demand
and therefore a distribution of income allowing some of those
who produced manufactured goods to buy a part of those
goods. This provided the economic base for nationalist-populist
political alliances among the bourgeoisie, the petty bourgeoisie, and at least a part of the organized workers' movement.
The policy of promoting goods for export does exactly the
opposite: domestic effective demand is of no interest for export
production; what is of interest is foreign demand, and therefore
the only important consideration is the cost of production,
which must be as low as possible. There is even competition
among underdeveloped countries to reduce production costs.
This results in a reduction of wages and an increase in exploitation and superexploitation—sheltered by a different kind of
political alliance. A sector of the local monopoly bourgeoisie,
integrated into international capital, increasingly produces for
the foreign market, either without developing capital to work
for the domestic market or by eliminating it (as in Chile). To
do this, it relies especially on the superexploitation of labor.
Thus the economic base for the kind of nationalist-populist
alliance, which existed under the import-substitution policy,
does not exist. Instead, there is a need to oppress the working
class and even a part of the bourgeoisie itself.

Superexploitation takes many forms. In the first place, capital
does not pay the worker a wage allowing the reproduction of
his or her labor power, which sometimes takes place within the
so-called noncapitalist sector. Such labor power thus becomes
integrated into the accumulation cycle via the classic emigra-
tion model, as in the case of South Africa and to a certain
extent Europe, where Spanish, Italian, and other workers
emigrate to the central economies. These workers can be
expelled when the business cycle so demands and can even be
thrown out when they are no longer sufficiently profitable.

In the case of economies like South Korea, Hong Kong, and
others, and especially in the free production zones, which
specialize in textiles and electronic components, work is
primarily done by women between the ages of fourteen and
twenty-four, who come from the countryside and who, after

working for a short time, are thrown out of the productive process again.

Superexploitation also takes place where there is an intensification of productive labor through extremely long work schedules. In Germany, for example, the average number of hours worked per year is between 1,700 and 1,800; in South Korea it is 2,800; in Malaysia it is 2,500. I want to stress, however, that 2,800 hours per year is an average for a country like South Korea; it is common to find people who work sixty, seventy, and even eighty-four hours a week (twelve hours a day, seven days a week) until they die or lose the ability to work. Then they are thrown out and replaced by others who can work at that pace. On the other hand, intensification in the strict sense of the word also takes place: the push to increase hourly output.

This obviously has an effect on the accident rate, which in a certain sense is both an index of superexploitation and a part of it. In 1971 in Brazil, for example, 18 percent of the economically active population suffered from work-related accidents; in 1972 this figure went up to 19 percent; in 1973 it was 20 percent; and in 1974 almost 22 percent of insured Brazilian workers had some type of accident at work. Fatal accidents rose at an increasingly rapid rate. An average of 25 percent work-related accidents means that a worker who works four years can expect to have an accident at work which is serious enough to be registered by the government's statistical services. There are various indications that the real accident rate is even higher. These work-related accidents occur because capitalists do not take security precautions—measures which are clearly not in their interests—and because the long hours and intensity of the work is such that the worker is not sufficiently rested, fed, or attentive.

Finally, superexploitation can be seen in the decline of real wages. This is happening in Brazil, where the real wage has fallen 40 percent since the military coup. In Argentina, the reduction in real wages since 1975 has been between 60 and 70 percent; in less than a year since the coup, there has been a 40 percent drop. In Chile real wages have fallen more than 50 percent since the military coup, to between 28 and 30 percent of their 1972 value.

To carry out this kind of superexploitation, it is clearly necessary to have a political regime that allows it. For example, in December 1971 the government of South Korea introduced a series of emergency measures, including a prohibition of strikes; since then the penalty for striking has been seven years in prison. The case of the Philippines is also important. In his own words: "I, Fernando Marcos, president of the Philippines, by virtue of the power invested in me by the Constitution, decide and decree the following: Section I: It is the policy of the State to support trade unionism and collective bargaining within the framework of compulsory arbitration . . . thus, all forms of strikes, pickets, and lockouts are strictly prohibited." Repressive laws of this type are appearing in most under-developed countries. The first measure the new military junta took in Thailand after the October 1976 coup was to prohibit all strikes and imprison the union leaders. Even in Egypt, following his new pro-Western stance after 1972, Sadat decreed life imprisonment for anyone who took part in a strike and damaged public or private property. In India, the first measure that Indira Gandhi took after adopting the state of emergency in June 1975 was to declare all strikes illegal: the number of work hours classified "lost for strikes" fell by 83 percent as compared to the preceding year. Other such provisions can be found on the African continent, where strikes are prohibited in more and more countries and political repression is on the rise. For example, in its 1975–1976 report, Amnesty International gave details of political repression (in one or more of the four categories they distinguish) in twenty-two African countries. The Latin American cases are sufficiently well known. The repressive laws of the military juntas in the Southern Cone are of the same type.

Even though in one sense all this repression is conjunctural, in another sense it is increasingly structural. It requires the erection of a political and economic state apparatus, based on an alliance of classes, that can establish a regime capable of making it possible for the underdeveloped country to fit into the international division of labor. We might call this form of state a technocratic-military state (others call it postcolonial or bureaucratic-capitalist and, I think incorrectly, semi- or neofascist state). The military juntas of Pinochet and Videla are the best known, but certainly not the only, examples. It is a tendency which is seen across the underdeveloped world: a repressive state based principally on military force, in which military commands become almost the backbone of the bourgeois state, producing an almost complete militarization of the society.

The very development of this type of state requires a new legitimating ideology—the "national security" ideology. I quote here the following note which the Bolivian news agency took from the *Estado de São Paulo* of August 6, 1976:

> The Brazilian military regime has served as the model for a new geopolitical concept of the state, which has already been adopted in various Latin American countries. It is principally based on the ideas of General Costa e Silva, chief of the president's civilian cabinet. This new model begins with the militarization of the powers which characterized the traditional state in the West, meaning the legislature, which is decorative, and the judiciary, which is not important. . . . The people is a myth; there are only nations and the nation is the state. . . . War is part of the human condition and all nations live in a state of war. All economic, cultural, and other activities are acts of war for or against the nation. As a consequence, we must strengthen military power as a guarantee of national security. The citizen must understand that security is more important than welfare, and that it is also necessary to sacrifice individual liberty. The armed forces would be the national elite responsible for running the state, and this is justified in Latin America by the volatility of the demagogic and corrupt civilians and by the requirements of war.

In addition, I quote Augusto Pinochet, a sufficiently well-known world "authority":

> National security is the responsibility of each and every Chilean; therefore, this concept must be inculcated at all socioeconomic levels through knowledge of general civic duties. Specifically

in relation to the domestic arena, we must encourage patriotic
values by disseminating our own cultural achievements in the
variegated gamut of native art, and by teaching and constantly
commenting on historical traditions and the respect for the
past which the fatherland represents for us.

All this serves to inculcate the new "national security"
ideology, which is no longer solely the patrimony of Brazil and
Chile. Now it is applied in a dozen Latin American states,
where "national security" provisions already cover a diverse
range of activities—as Pinochet says, economic, political, and
cultural activities. And this is happening not only in Latin
America, but increasingly in Asia, the Middle East, and Africa.
Technocratic-military states vest themselves in the new "national security" ideology designed, insofar as is possible, to
legitimate the regime domestically and give it international
credence as well. These strong-arm regimes, their national
security ideologies, their domestically repressive and externally
bellicose policies, their subservience to imperialism become
necessary in order to put into effect the new international
division of labor, which, in turn, was provoked by the world
capital accumulation crisis currently underway.

In conclusion, I would like to go back and refer to the major
industrialized Western countries. Although they still have not
reached this degree of repression and do not yet have governments of "national unity" or "national salvation," their austerity
policies seem to be leading in the same direction. They are
calling upon everyone to sacrifice for the national common
good in order to cover up what capital is imposing on the
working class. This situation tends to create the conditions for
the establishment of increasingly repressive political regimes.
The degree to which capital will succeed in imposing them
clearly depends on the direction the class struggle will take,
and on the bourgeoisie's ability to make the working class,
through its reformist political organizations, allow, or even
collaborate in, the bourgeoisie's austerity policy.

On the other hand, this evolution will be different if the
working class does not accept this austerity policy and does not

allow capital to restructure itself and recover, thus impeding the new international division of labor that the bourgeoisie is determined to impose on us. This depends on the working class's decision to struggle until the final victory.

6. THE ECONOMICS OF CRISIS
AND THE CRISIS OF ECONOMICS

Economic Astrology: The Crystal Ball Is Clouded

The problem of inflation has been defeated . . . the danger of any recession is nil.
> —Gerald Ford, March 17, 1970

Let us pledge together to make these next four years the best four years in America's history, so that on its 200th birthday America will be as young and vital as when it began, and as bright a beacon of hope to the world. Let us go forward from here confident in hope, strong in our faith in one another, sustained by our faith in God who created us, and striving always to serve his purposes.
> —Richard Nixon, Inaugural Address, January 20, 1973

No law of the market compels a market economy to suffer from recessions or periodic inflations.
> —Lyndon Johnson, *Economic Report of the President,* 1965

The National Bureau of Economic Research has worked itself out of one of its first jobs, namely business cycles.
> —Paul Samuelson, Nobel Laureate in Economics,
> September 24, 1970

A public opinion poll showed that Americans ranked the forecasting ability of economists just about on a par with that of astrologers.
> —*Fortune,* January 1976

This is a revised version of an article that appeared in *Critique* 9: 85–112, 1978. It was originally drafted in 1976 as the opening chapters of *Crisis: In the World Economy.*

History is witness to the moral worth and scientific accuracy of the pious hopes and predictions of political leaders and their economic advisors. It is hardly necessary to recall that as late in his reign as April 1974 Richard Nixon predicted that "1975 will be a very good year, and 1976 the richest in American history." Following its first defeat in a war at the hands of the Vietnamese, and the first resignation of one of its presidents, with nearly 10 percent unemployed and a rate of inflation of over 10 percent, the United States led the "free world" into the most severe economic crisis of a generation.

Nothing compels a market economy to suffer recession and inflation, claimed Lyndon Johnson, but it was only his own escalation of the war against Vietnam that postponed the recession in the United States (though not in Germany and elsewhere) until the end of the 1960s, and it was Johnson's, and subsequently Nixon's, policy of global deficit finance— creating tens of billions of unrequited dollars that the rest of the world came to hold after supplying the United States with materials and selling them their industries—that launched the worldwide inflation. In a vain attempt to keep the economic and political wolf from the door, the world economy became saturated with money, the balance of payments deteriorated, foreign debts increased dangerously, and the private sector's debt-equity ratio rose even more dangerously. A classical overproduction crisis of accumulation developed, and the general rate of profit declined. The value of the dollar and the stability of the world monetary system were sacrificed to the scramble for shares in a declining market, amid mutual recriminations about economic irresponsbility. Thus the capitalist world fell into its severest postwar recession, with declines of production up to 10 and 15 percent in 1974–1975 (really beginning in mid-1973, *before* the oil crisis). The recovery in 1976 has not eliminated unemployment and does not, according to capital's most authorized political and economic spokesmen, promise to do so before the end of the decade, by which time we may expect a recession more severe than the one just past. In other words, despite the pious hopes of political leadership and the predictions of economic advisors, the world capitalist economy is again visited by a major crisis of accumulation, and such political leaders as Henry Kissinger (at the United Nations General Assembly on September 23, 1974) and Harold Wilson have now turned (or did during the 1974–1975 recession) to foreboding shades of the great depression of the 1930s. Even if this foreboding may be more appropriate than the earlier optimism, the basis of such latter-day predictions is, at least as far as their scientific advisors are concerned, as unfounded and shaky as ever.

Paul Samuelson—professor of economics at the Massachusetts Institute of Technology, author of the most widely used textbook in economics, co-author of a biweekly column in *Newsweek,* advisor (by his own account) to "some large institutional investors," advisor to US presidents (who offered him the chairmanship of the Council of Economic Advisors), winner of the Nobel Prize for economics—is not alone among professional economists in having claimed (as recently as 1970!) that the most prestigious scientific institution for business cycle research in the United States and perhaps the world had worked itself out of a job. Nor is he alone among economists in patting himself on the back when referring to the supposed obsolescence of the business cycle and the need to "redefine . . . the pre-war dinosaur [as] a post-war lizard." "I predicted this would happen," he stated.[1] Alexander Eckstein, scientific board member of the National Bureau of Economic Research (NBER), offered the opinion that "given the values of society, the probability of a traditional recession with unemployment of 7 percent is fairly low."[2] Only five years later official unemployment in the United States had risen to nearly 10 percent (and by some unofficial estimates to double that figure). In July 1976 it stood at more than 7 percent and is expected to remain above that level for years! A more cautious opinion was voiced at the same colloquium by Solomon Fabricant, an expert in long-term growth and productivity trends: "The causes of the business cycle have not vanished. . . . A tiger cage is not the same as a tiger loose in the streets, but neither is it a paper tiger."[3] Accepting Fabricant's sinophylism, we may ask *who* has caged the tiger which in 1975 leaves 17 million workers officially (and in reality), unemployed, with many more than that loose on the streets of Organization for Economic Cooperation and Development (OECD) member countries alone? What kind of economic "science" leads to such picturesque predictions—and supports such ineffectual, cagey, economic policy?

The American Economic Association (AEA), at its annual meeting in December 1973, invited a number of its most prestigious economists to participate in a panel to ponder the "major economic problems of the 1970's—the clouded crystal ball." The list of problems offered by Kermit Gordon, president of the Brookings Institution, included (1) international economic problems, (2) inflation, (3) performance of the public sector, (4) distributive equity, and (5) environment, energy, resource development, growth.[4] Though the 1973–1975 recession had already started, unemployment—let alone recession or depression or economic crisis—did not appear on this list of problems at all. The crystal ball was clouded indeed!

Geoffrey Moore, vice-president for research of the NBER and a renowned expert in the study of business cycles and their history, compared the pattern of recession in the 1948–1970 period with that in the 1920–1938 period (but without giving any persuasive reason for selecting this latter point of reference) and came to the conclusion that business recessions have become less frequent, shorter, and milder due to the shift in industrial composition to more stable sectors such as services. Therefore, he argued, "future recessions are more likely to be in the nature of slowdowns in the rate of economic growth" rather than downturns, and the "trend does not seem to show up in the level of the unemployment rate."[5]

Robert Heilbroner used the same occasion to strengthen his foresight with hindsight. Recalling prominent features of the preceding two decades, such as the multinational corporation, Japan, economic development in the Third World, inflation, environment, and so forth, Heilbroner observed:

> *Every one of these problems was invisible in the 1950's.* In point of fact, had I really been holding forth on the outlook in the early 1950's, I doubt that I would have mentioned a single one of them. For in those years, it was not growth but the threat of

chronic recession that still absorbed the attention of the profession. Inflation was a matter on which no sessions were
organized, because we knew that it could not occur as long as
unemployment was 4 or 5 percent of the labor force.[6]

And such unemployment has become "obsolete" since then!
Heilbroner continued:

> Like everyone else, I have my list of expected policy issues
> of the 1970's—a "surprise-free" list, in Herman Kahn's ter-
> minology. It includes the very problems I have just enumerated:
> growth, inflation, the environment, the multinationals, the
> failure of development, the international monetary situation.
> But I am moved to ask, reflecting on the past, whether this list
> of problems is likely to be as misconceived.

So Heilbroner, who has always been a bit of a maverick, pro-
ceeded to make some presumably not so surprising predictions
of the major economic problems of the 1970s: (1) increasing
microbreakdown, disfunction, even nonfuction of *parts* of the
system rather than of its main macroaggregates; (2) increased
tension over income *distribution* and the reappearance of
Disraeli's "vanished" war of the rich against the poor; and (3)
decline of neoclassical theory, more *institutional* [certainly
maximizing] behavior as the object of the theory of economic
policy. Not so surprising indeed!

Neither his reflections on the past, nor his experience of the
current crisis, led Heilbroner to make any mention at all of
unemployment, let alone of "chronic recession" that he said
had once absorbed the profession. Clouded crystal ball? The
august members of the AEA, leaders of the profession, cannot
even see the reality before them: disfunction of microparts,
certainly not of large macroaggregates, let alone of the system
as a whole. Who else would be fooled by this professional
gobbledygook than other economists? Tension over distribution but no class struggle over power? And what is on the
horizon for the profession's theory of economic policy? The
replacement of microanalysis by institutional description! God
forbid the monopoly corporations to seek to maximize profits
or minimize losses. Unfortunately, they do not listen to God
but only to the ringing of the cash register, the ticker of the

tape, and the hum of the computer, which spell out the
balance sheet of profit and loss. No recognition here that it
is the monopoly structure of the economy that permits the
impossible—inflation with unemployment—let alone the fact
that the process of accumulation and disaccumulation now
requires 10 percent inflation and 10 percent unemployment
(perhaps even 20 percent of one or the other or both: Britain,
Italy, and Japan have already reached annual levels of inflation
of 25 percent). There is no problem here, no call for the
revision or redirection of neoclassical micro- and of Keynesian
macrotheory to analyze international monopoly state capitalism
on the micro and macro, or macro-micro, level.

The professors of economics are not alone in their total
failure to predict the future, or even to recognize the past.
Business Week editorialized in its special issue of September
14, 1974:

> Five years ago, the editors of *Business Week* looked ahead to the
> decade of the 1970's and devoted a special issue to an analysis
> of the forces that would be shaping the U.S. economy. They
> foresaw a period of vigorous economic growth. . . . The first
> five years of the seventies have confirmed these forecasts. It is
> indeed a "super" decade.

Nonetheless, the editors now observe four "unforeseen developments . . . where the forecasters underestimated the
magnitude of the developments at work": the development of
a cartel of oil-producing countries, inflationary expansion, the
scale of indicative government intervention, and the enormous
total of capital demand:

> The most striking characteristic of the world economy today is
> its inflationary bias . . . [the] more important reason is the
> worldwide commitment to full employment and maximum
> production. . . . The industrial nations . . . resolved that they
> would never again go through a major economic contraction.
> Over the years, they developed a pattern of responding auto-
> matically to any sign of weakness with huge doses of deficit
> spending and easy money. The response has worked.

Literally unbelievable! At the time of this issue unemployment
in the "industrialized nations" had already risen by several

million, and less than twelve months later it reached 17 million.
What worldwide commitment to full employment? Where
were the automatic responses to any sign of weakness? What
responses have worked—and for whom? And that was in
September 1974!

Fortune, the most prestigious and authorative business journal in the United States, in its monthly "Business Roundup"
for July 1974 still predicted:

> By comparison with the past eighteen months, the next eighteen
> will seem almost sunny. . . . Industrial production will rise at
> an average rate of a bit under 4 percent over the coming
> eighteen months . . . the world doesn't seem to be moving into
> a severe recession . . . unemployment will tend to increase to
> just below 6 percent.

By October 1974, a month after *Business Week* had given
the economy a clean bill of health, *Fortune* cautiously revised
its "Business Roundup" estimate: "The risk of the unusual
or unexpected—such as might produce a serious or prolonged
recession—are perhaps greater than at any other time in
postwar history. And they have to be taken more seriously
now." Halfway through the most prolonged US recession
in postwar history, *Fortune* was only just beginning to pull
its head out of the sand. November's "Business Roundup,"
now entitled "The Real Recession Is Yet to Come," observed
that "the disagreement between President Ford, who says that
we're not in a recession, and Federal Reserve Chairman
Arthur Burns, who says that we are, reflects the peculiarity
of our situation . . . we haven't thus far had the *feel* of a
recession." But, reported *Fortune* in the same article, "Of the
250 executives reporting to *Fortune*'s semi-annual sampling of
the business mood, two out of three—but they looked for an
upturn in 1975—are not worried, rather than confident about
the outlook."

According to *Newsweek,* October 28, 1974, a Gallup poll
reported 51 percent of the American people thought they
were moving into a depression. Finally, at the end of November
the US Treasury Secretary admitted that this was the worst
recession since the war (*Financial Times,* November 30, 1974).

Nonetheless, *Foreign Affairs,* the most authoritative oracle of the US political establishment, published articles in January 1975 in which Harold Cleveland and Bruce Brittain, the monetarist disciples of Milton Friedman, answered the question, A world depression? with a large No, assuring us that the Great Depression of the 1930s was caused by a contraction of the money supply, that the current recession can be managed successfully, and that the key questions today are world inflation and world money. By that time unemployment had risen to some 10 million. In the same issue of *Foreign Affairs,* Hollis Chenery, vice-president of the World Bank and director of its development planning, published an article entitled "Restructuring the World Economy," in which the only problems mentioned were increases in prices of oil and food; the restructuring implicit in, and necessitated by, the crisis of capital accumulation went without mention.

Not even the shortest of short-term prediction is any more realistic. By February 1975, the official unemployment rate in the United States had risen to 8.2 percent. The government claimed it would *not* pass 8.5 percent, but would hover around 8 percent until 1977. Only two months later the unemployment rate had risen to 8.9 percent, and then 9.2 percent in May.

Other governments, international organizations such as OECD, economic and "cycle" research institutes, as well as the major organs of the press (except for the *Economist*) do not have a better record. Thus on July 1, 1974, the London *Times* predicted that the United States, Germany, France, Britain, Italy, and Japan together would show a growth of 0.5 percent for 1974 and that they would go on to grow by 3.7 percent in 1975. In fact, in that period production in these countries *declined* by over 10 percent. The HWWA Institute in Hamburg predicted that world trade would grow by 6 percent in 1974 and 5 percent in 1975. In fact, it *suffered a real decline of 10 percent* in 1975. The French national plan for 1971–1975, which traditionally is little more than an expression of the needs and desires of business, projected growth rates of 5.9 percent for GNP, 6.8 percent for productive investment, and 3 percent for value added for 1971–1975. The real rates achieved were 3.6 percent, 3.6 percent, and 0.9 percent respectively.

Even predictions of future rates of inflation have not been even moderately accurate. Table 1 gives the rates of inflation predicted each year for the next by the US Council of Economic Advisors, compared with the actual figures:

Table 1. Predicted and actual rates of inflation, 1968–1974

Year	Predicted inflation	Real inflation	Difference	% excess of real over predicted
1968	3.1	3.9	0.8	26
1969	3.0	4.8	1.8	60
1970	4.8	5.5	0.7	14
1971*	3.0	4.5	1.5	50
1972	3.2	3.4	0.2	6
1973	3.0	5.5	2.5	73
1974	7.0	12.0	5.0	71
1968–1974 average				43

*During part of 1971 and 1972 there was price control.

But at least contemporary economists are true to form. If today's practitioners of the dismal science are a dismal failure at prediction, they are only following in the footsteps of their predecessors. Thus as Joseph S. Davis recalls:

> Poor vision was extremely prevalent in the late 1920's and persisted in the 1930's, in a great many respects, of which I only select one. Keynes wrote in August 1931: "Banks and bankers are by nature blind. They have not seen what was coming." This extreme statement, whatever its degree of truth, was pointed too narrowly. Though he had better vision than most, even Keynes failed to see what was coming. So did Einzig, a well-informed and perspicacious financial writer. . . . Time and again respected analysts overlooked or underweighted signs of weakness or danger, went wrong in their forecasts, omitted or muted timely warnings, and evinced ill-founded hopes. . . . If Keynes sensed the menace of Hitler and Nazism, I have looked in vain for evidence of it.[7]

Of the stockmarket crash of 1929, he wrote:

On the other side of the Atlantic, America's most respected economist, Irving Fisher, on October 15 [1929] had asserted that stock prices were on "a permanently high plateau." On October 23 he assured the District of Columbia Banker's Association that the market decline was only temporary. On November 3 he expressed the view that unexampled prosperity had justified the stock market boom, that foolish panic was responsible for the recent crash, and that prices were absurdly low; and he foresaw no break in the nation's record prosperity. On November 6 John D. Rockefeller was reported as saying that the destruction of security values was unjustified and that he and his son were buying substantial amounts of stock.[8]

In 1928 and 1929 the NBER and other prominent economists prepared an exhaustive report, entitled *Recent Economic Changes,* for the US government. Despite some reservations about future prospects by NBER Director Wesley C. Mitchel late in 1930, a reviewer looked back and observed that "nowhere in the 943 pages is there any strong suggestion that the crisis of late 1929 was blowing up."[9]

A decade later, Joseph Schumpeter would look back defensively:

> It is of the utmost importance to realize this: given the facts which it was then possible for either businessmen or economists to observe, those diagnoses . . . were not simply wrong. What nobody saw, though some people may have felt it, was that those fundamental data from which diagnoses and prognoses were made, were themselves in a state of flux. . . . People, for the most part, stood their ground firmly. But the ground itself was about to give way.[10]

While the economic and political ground was giving way under his feet, President Hoover continued to insist that prosperity was greater and firmer than ever—and he put political pressure on economists from the NBER and elsewhere to reflect this ill-founded political optimism in their scientific diagnoses and predictions.[11]

In the face of this dismal predictive record the innocent layman—and other "professional" economists as well—may be tempted to suppose that much of this misplaced emphasis, ill-founded optimism, and seemingly counterproductive prediction is the result of mixing immediate, political convenience, business rationale, or even just plain good human spirits with hard, positive economic science. Moreover, our review above is admittedly a mixed bag of nonrandom samples of all kinds of predictive techniques and nontechniques. In that case, one might innocently expect that the new, hardnosed, professional econometric model-builders (backed up by computers and armies of graduate students to do all the empirical dirty work, handsomely paid with retainers and contracts from corporations and government departments that need hard facts and not flimsy wishes) would be significantly more successful with the predictions that their computers derive from their thousands of equations. But in March 1975 (p. 157), *Fortune* writes, under the subtitle, "But Does It Really Work?":

> Given the vast prestige and commercial success of econometric models, it might be assumed that their superiority over conventional forecasting methods is firmly established. Oddly enough, it isn't at all established. Consider, for example, the record of the econometric models in forecasting last year's economy. At the end of 1973, Wharton was projecting a 0.6 percent increase in real growth for 1974 and a 7.2 percent increase in GNP prices. Chase weighed in with a forecast of 0.7 percent real growth and a 6.6 percent increase in prices. DRI had a 1.2 percent growth in output and a 6.5 percent price rise. In fact, real GNP actually declined by 2.2 percent last year and prices rose by 10.2 percent. Thus Wharton did the best of the three models—which still wasn't very good. . . . But when McNees compared the forecasts of the models with those made in the same period (1970–1973) by 36 economists who relied primarily on their judgment, he found that neither method was proved superior.

And what "judgment," if any, our economists have and merit, we have already seen above.

Under these circumstances, we should *not* be in for any surprises if we take a closer, timely, and politically interesting look at the predictions of the designer and director of Wharton, which did the "best of the three models." He is Lawrence R. Klein, who "heads a task force advising Mr. Carter on the economy, [and who] is in frequent touch with the Democratic candidate." In the August 23, 1976, issue of *U.S. News & World Report,* he answered this question:

> Q. Professor Klein, is the economic recovery in the U.S. fizzling out? A. No. We are in the middle of the recovery—and not a bad recovery. Economic growth slowed a bit in the second quarter, but it will pick up again later this year. Q. How long will the expansion last? A. If you mean "When will we see a decline in economic activity?" nothing like that can be foreseen at this point. But less-than-normal growth seems in store for 1978. By that I mean we can look for a natural inventory adjustment, and industry will be bumping up against some capacity ceilings, resulting in a fresh inflationary thrust. Calculations made by some economists also allow for a rather slow recovery in the rest of the world, but the projections I've seen recently say that, for the rest of the world, 1977 looks pretty good. And for the rest of the world at least, 1978 looks even better.

A month earlier (July 19, 1976) the same magazine cited Klein as saying that with "proper government policies this period of expansion could turn out to be a replay of the 1960's boom."

Klein was not alone in his bullish optimism. The July 19 issue carried another optimistic article under the title "Experts' View: Business to Climb for Years to Come":

> The business recovery under way for 15 months will be a healthy one that will run into 1977, at the least, and perhaps well beyond that. The torrid pace of recent growth will slow. But it's not until late 1977 or early 1978 that the experts see any big problems at all. . . . But most economists expect that any correction that follows will be short and modest. And many analysts are placing bets that the U.S. is in the early stages of an expansion that could stretch nearly to the end of the decade, a long upsurge much like the boom of the 1960's. Economists at New York Citibank have reached this bullish conclusion: "The current expansion is most likely to last through 1978 and probably longer, and . . . any recession that

may occur before the end of the decade is likely to be milder than the one the U.S. economy is now shedding."

It should come as no surprise that this bullish optimism was not warranted either in fact or in theory. In fact, unemployment in the United States began to rise in June 1976 (from 7.2 percent in May) and has continued to rise up until November (when it stood at 8.1 percent). Since late summer 1973, unemployment has also begun to rise again in Germany, France, and Japan, not to mention England and Italy, where it has continued its upward path throughout the "recovery." For the European Economic Community as a whole, unemployment also stopped declining and began rising in June 1976 (*International Herald Tribune,* August 17, 1976). By September it had reached 5.7 percent in Holland and 8.7 percent in Belgium (*Le Monde,* November 13, 1976), up to 9.4 percent in November (*Frankfurter Rundschau,* December 13, 1976). Of course, maintaining employment is not the most significant criterion for capital. But output and the "leading economic indicators" generally also slowed down or fell by summer 1976. In the United States the index of leading economic indicators *declined* in August and September and failed to rise in October 1976. Moreover, as *U.S. News & World Report* (August 16, 1976) points out about this composite index of twelve economic series designed for economic prediction, "Sometimes the indicators are laggards, not leaders." In Germany and Japan, where industrial production fell in August and September, the recovery petered out. This is what the OECD *Economic Outlook* (p. 13), published in December 1976, said:

> The recovery which began in North America in mid-1975 and then spread to Europe and Japan . . . was always expected to lose pace in the second half of 1976. In fact, the latest indicators suggest that the slowdown not only began sooner, but has been appreciably greater, than suggested in the July *Economic Outlook.* The slowdown is widespread, affecting virtually all OECD countries, and the expansion in the United States and Japan in particular is less than expected. Expansion in Europe can best be described as modest. . . . In the seven major economies taken together, industrial output has stagnated since April.

In the United States it continued to pick up until September, but in Japan, Germany, the United Kingdom and Canada it has been about flat since midyear and in France it has slowed down markedly since the first quarter. . . . Aggregate GNP for the seven major OECD countries is estimated to have been expanding in the second half of 1976 at an annual level of 3.5 percent, substantially less than the forecast of 4.75 percent contained in the July issue of *Economic Outlook.* Total unemployment has, accordingly, started to rise again.

By October 25, 1976, *U.S. News & World Report,* which in July had announced "business to climb for years to come" according to the "experts," published a survey of "top business economists for major U.S. companies." According to 6 percent of those surveyed, the next economic downturn would begin in 1977, in 1978 according to 54 percent, in 1979 according to 25 percent, in 1980 according to 4 percent, and after that according to 8 percent. "Expert" opinions change fast, but not as fast as events!

Yet there are good reasons in the theory of business cycles and in the analysis of capital accumulation that could and "should" have led to serious doubts about the bullish optimism (or the equally unanalytic subsequent gloom). The most important facts relating to this theory and analysis were available at the time these optimistic forecasts were made, and some of the above-cited forecasters even mentioned some of these facts, apparently without realizing, or at least taking account of, their significance. The most important of these facts refer to investment and to such significant indicators of investment as the demand for steel. Thus, in his August interview in *U.S. News & World Report,* Klein noted,

> If you analyze the present recovery, it's definitely consumer-led. There's a lot of . . . rebuilding of inventories, and these forces are somewhat transitory. . . . You have to remember that a lot of investment, instead of raising capacity, is now directed at energy problems, and they're going to take a long time to solve. And a lot of investment is directed toward protecting the environment.

Indeed, in the very July article which confidently announced the "climb for years to come," *U.S. News & World Report* observed, apparently without understanding its significance, the absence of

> a widely predicted burst of business spending on new plants and equipment [which] should sustain economic growth for a still longer period. Such a surge in capital investment is long overdue, if past upturns are an accurate guide. After adjusting for inflation, this type of investment is considerably lower today than it was when the economy touched bottom in early 1975. This is the first time in the postwar era that that has been true in the advanced stage of recovery.

In Britain, productive investment declined absolutely in 1974, 1975, and 1976, and is now £1.66 million compared to £2.13 million in 1970 (*Financial Times,* October 5, 1976). The Japanese recovery was export-led (and therefore dependent on recovery elsewhere). As to the investment-sensitive and indicative steel industry, *Financial Times* reported, "The French steel industry. A deep depression. . . . W. German rolled steel orders show further fall" (November 19, 1976).

The poor investment picture is in part due to relatively depressed profits and low expectations of profitability, although thanks to recent economic management, profits are on the rise again, particularly for big monopoly business. The more immediate reasons are excess installed, or underutilized, productive capacity, with estimated utilization rates of between 74 percent and 82 percent in the United States and 80 percent in Britain, Italy, and Japan (Ernest Mandel in *Inprecor* [Italy], November 11, 1976, p. 6), and the direction of "new" investment in the major industrialized economies toward rationalization designed to reduce (labor) costs of production at existing capacity rather than to increase capacity.

Yet we may venture to "predict" that it is precisely this slack—rather than lag—in investment that is the significant and decisive factor in the present weak cyclical recovery. I believe that this lack of investment, without which consumer buying and inventory buildups cannot sustain a boom, is a reflection of the deepgoing crisis of accumulation that has been brewing since the mid-1960s and of which the 1960–1970 and the 1973–1975 recessions were only early stages, with more and deeper recessions to come. Be that as it may, elsewhere in the capitalist world it is clear that major investment is not so much "overdue" as unlikely until far-reaching political and economic changes have occurred. Thus *Economic Outlook* for December 1975 observed and predicted more realistically:

> The enormous amount of slack built up in the OECD area since the beginning of the downturn will not start being reabsorbed over the forecast period; the margin of unused resources would at best stabilize in the course of 1976. . . . What is shown is a recovery from recession which results largely from a fiscal boost to demand and an end to the run-down of inventories. Both factors are forecast to lose force in the course of 1976. . . . Business fixed investment seems unlikely to become a major factor of strength . . . personal savings rate is now extremely high . . . the recovery is envisaged as faltering for some countries.

Official sources, business economists, economic research institutes, and even some politicians in Germany, France, Britain, and Japan all suggest that there is no immediate prospect for a recovery of *investment* and that the unemployment created by the recession of 1972–1975 is not likely to be eliminated by the "recovery" of 1976 or 1977 or 1978, even if it lasts that long—which is very unlikely if investment does not pick up and unemployment persists.

Under the circumstances, it is difficult to find anything more than misplaced professional pride in the ex-chairman of the Council of Economic Advisors, Walter Heller, when he asked, What's right with economics? and assured himself and his audience that we economists "have many sins, none deadly, to confess, but these are far outweighed by the virtues, all quite lively, that we can legitimately profess."[12] Yet Heller observes what Gunnar Myrdal and Robert Heilbroner charge, that being behind the times is the regular methodological weakness of establishment economists. And Heller notes that "inflation may no longer be the Public Enemy Number One now that severe recession is upon us, but it is surely Economists' Enemy Number One." Nonetheless, Heller makes so bold as to claim that "in a very real sense economists have been victims of their own success. Macroeconomic policy was the major force holding the postwar economy on a vastly higher plane than the prewar economy." Only "Vietnam blew the economy off course" and it is a fault that the economics profession has "not satisfactorily explained [or caged] stagflation."[13] Shades of Samuelson's congratulations to the NBER except that Heller has the temerity to congratulate his colleagues and himself for having caged the tiger through macroeconomic policy, citing Vietnam as only an extraneous gale on the course his economists have steered! And that in the face of having escalated the war against Vietnam and financed it as the *macroeconomic* policy, specifically to cage or at least export the tiger of the deepening crisis of capital accumulation while it was still a young cub in the mid-1960s and before it broke out to roam the streets, alleys, and country lanes of the world in the 1970s. But before proceeding to examine this crisis itself, we may perhaps appropriately evaluate the claim that one of the lively virtues of economists is to have invented and invoked macroeconomic policy, and that it was this policy that kept the economy riding high, at least until now. Like the economists' predictions, it will be seen that none of these explicit and implicit claims have any basis in reality!

Economic Management: Keynesian Class Policy

Walter Heller's statement that "macroeconomic policy was the major force holding the postwar economy on a vastly higher plane than the prewar economy" is belied by any objective examination of the economic record before and after World War II. The proposition, implicit in this claim and explicit in many similar statements, that class-neutral government economic policy, based on Keynesian theory, can and does assure steady economic growth without unemployment or inflation in the capitalist industrial countries (and that it could do the same in the underdeveloped countries) is contrary both to the visible evidence and to any acceptable theory of the capitalist process of capital accumulation.

Similarly, Paul Samuelson wrote in the fourth edition of his *Economics:*

> Here at the end of Part Two's analysis of aggregative economics or macroeconomics, it is fitting to formulate an important tenet of modern economics. *Neoclassical synthesis: by means of appropriately reinforcing monetary and fiscal policies, our mixed-enterprise system can avoid the excesses of boom and slump and can look forward to healthy progressive growth.*[14]

To begin with, "Keynesian," public, countercyclical, macroeconomic stabilization and growth policy has been practiced, as Keynes himself observed, throughout history, and it never assured sustained noncyclical growth before. More particularly, as Marc Blaug has noted:

> The leaders of the American profession strongly supported a programme of public works and specifically attacked the shibboleth of a balanced budget. A long list of names, including Slichter, Taussig, Schultz, Yntema, Simons, Gayer, Knight, Vinr, Douglas and J. M. Clark, concentrated mainly at the universities of Chicago and Columbia but with allies in other universities, research foundations, and government and banking circles, declared themselves in print well before 1936 [the year in which Keynes' *General Theory* was published] in favour of policies that we would today call Keynesian. Similarly, in England, as Hutchison has shown, names such as Pigou, Layton, Stamp, Harrod, Gaitskell, Meade, E. A. G. and J. Robinson came out publicly in favour of compensatory public spending. . . . A fair way of summarizing the evidence is to say that most economists, at least in the English-speaking countries, were united in respect of practical measures for dealing with depression, but were utterly disunited in respect of the theory that lay behind these policy conclusions. . . . In a sense, then, the Keynesian theory succeeded because it produced the policy conclusions most economists wanted to advocate anyway, but it produced these as logical inferences from a tightly knit theory.[15]

The application of "Keynesian" macroeconomic remedies both before Keynes and after did not heal the economic patient or permit its healthy progressive growth before World War II, so it is not clear why such a policy should be expected (and immediately after the war it was not!) to produce, or now be credited with producing, healthy growth on a high plane since the war. Indeed, in the United States it was the war itself that eliminated the 10 million unemployed and "healed" the economy. In Germany, Italy, and Japan it was the "Keynesian" plus fascist policies of Hitler, Mussolini, and Tojo, based on repression at home—especially of the wage rate—and expansion abroad, that spurred capital accumulation on again. Only Britain, which had preceded the rest of the world into depression in the 1920s, enjoyed an earlier cyclical recovery, although clearly not because of Keynes or macroeconomics, while suffering from ever increasing structural depression and the loss of its world leadership to the United States. Indeed, it was US accession to world economic, political, and military dominance, assisted by the effects of the depression (and the ineffectiveness of Keynesian macroeconomics in overcoming it) and the war on rival powers that lifted and held the US economy to a relatively higher plane after the war, and not postwar Keynesian macroeconomic policy.

Beyond its temporary ability to support "healthy progressive growth" during the postwar years, largely derived from its position of dominance over rivals in the rest of the capitalist world, both developed and underdeveloped, US capital has prospered from the highly favorable relation to labor that had been wrought by the same depression, fascism, and war. The depression of the wage rate and the destruction of unions in Germany and Italy, and the social democratic containment of the labor movement in Italy, France, and Britain after the war, afforded enormous benefits first to US capital, during and after the Marshall Plan, and then to national capital (and still indirectly to US capital) in these countries. It was the conjunction of these relations with working-class and intercapitalist imperialist relations, helped along by the economic and physical destruction of capital by the depression and the war and the permanent war economy, that since the war has been supported by the artificially stimulated anti-Communist hysteria and then the arms race, that have permitted a massive new wave of capital investment and accumulation on a high plane in the postwar economy and not Keynesian macro-economic policy.

The thesis of high-level, healthy, progressive growth through macroeconomic policy in the postwar period is belied by fact and theory on several other grounds. For the United States, Steindl argued persuasively in the 1950s that prolonged expansion was no longer possible;[16] and Baran and Sweezy sought to explain how the tendencies toward stagnation began to assert themselves in the 1960s and were only being held at bay by wasteful, especially military, expenditure of the "economic surplus."[17] Since the mid-1960s the Kennedy–Johnson boom was prolonged and recession averted or postponed only through escalation of the war against Vietnam and an expansionary monetary policy that flooded the world with Eurodollars and lent the necessary monetary support to the subsequent inflations of the 1970s. However, this boom and inflation led capital and its representatives in government to accept—indeed to promote—recession, supposedly to fight inflation as public enemy number one.

Even the supposed "stabilizing" capacity and effects of macroeconomic policy are more than doubtful. Right-wing economists, such as Milton Friedman, who oppose the use of expansionary fiscal policy because it involves public expenditure that may benefit not only capital but also labor, have argued all along that fiscal policy cannot stabilize, and that because of lags between its implementation and its effect it often destabilizes the economy. Monetary policy, they claim, benefits capital more directly and exclusively and will serve not only to stabilize the economy but also to eliminate business cycle fluctuations. They even go so far as to claim that only an inappropriate and ill-timed decline in the money supply caused the Great Depression. But an increasing number of studies by left-wing and bourgeois economists show that macroeconomic fiscal and monetary policy do not and cannot stabilize, let alone eliminate, the cyclical fluctuations in the process of accumulation. The so-called built-in automatic stabilizers (such as taxes that go up in times of expansion and down in times of contraction) have more direct effects on consumption expenditures than on investment, which is the more important unstable factor in accumulation. Moreover, as the contemporary attack on welfare expenditures shows, some of these "automatic stabilizers" are automatically built out of the system again when the interests of capital demand it and the nonmilitancy of labor allows it. Discretionary macroeconomic stabilization policy is just that: it is exercised at the discretion of the powers that be and as a function of their economic and political interests. As long as economists have been unable to foresee the amplitude of the cyclical swings—much less to predict the cyclical turns—it is not surprising that they have also been unable to suggest policies to restrain that amplitude and prevent the downturns. At best, the swings have been dampened in some cases in some countries, but more often the stabilizing effects of macroeconomic policy have been marginal or nonexistent; and sometimes they have aggravated the cyclical swings. For instance, in every recession in the United States since 1948 federal employment declined, and in the intervening expansions it increased. Moreover, the stop-go policy, long practiced in Britain, which must accompany or dampen the fluctuations in the accumulation process, restricts the freedom of capital and discourages domestic investment, particularly where it is relatively easy for capital to move overseas.

The failure of macroeconomic stabilization policy is not, however, due only to problems of prediction and technical effectiveness. On the contrary, though capital and the capitalist state undoubtedly wish to use discretionary macroeconomic policy to prevent inflation and unemployment excesses, class interests are far from unambiguous, and inflation and unemployment are as much weapons to serve capital as problems it must avoid. This has clearly been the case with inflation, which capital has required and governments have been prepared to support—up to a point. Even the voice of American big business, *Fortune* (August 1974, p. 25) recognized that "in recent months, however, the real push behind these prices has come from businessmen straining to restore their profit margins." In fact, the evidence shows that the greater the threat to profits and the higher the degree of monopolization between industries or countries, the greater is the inflation induced by the former and made possible—with state acquiescence or support—by the latter.[19]

Thus, the recent worldwide inflation has been most severe precisely in those industrialized countries—in Britain, Italy, and Japan inflation reached a yearly rate of 25 percent—in which the rate of profit declined the most. Among the underdeveloped countries also the most severe inflationary takeoffs have occurred where capital has suffered the greatest decline in profits and the crisis of accumulation has become most severe. Similarly, as between industries in particular countries, price rises are most marked in industries that are most monopolized. Sherman shows that in the US recession years of 1953, 1958, and 1969, competitive prices rose 1.9 percent, 0.5 percent, and 5.9 percent respectively. In 1948, when the degree of monopolization was not yet as strong, competitive prices had fallen 7.8 percent and monopoly prices also went down, although by much less—only 1.9 percent. This inflationary behavior of monopoly prices compared to competitive prices has occurred despite the fact that in the recessions between 1947 and 1965 profits in monopolized industries only declined 26.7 percent on the average, while in competitive industries they declined 51.7 percent, and in the smaller industries with less than $250,000 in assets they fell on average by 82.7 percent.[20]

John M. Blair wrote in the *Journal of Economic Issues* (June 1974):

> The weighted average price change in the recession of December 1969–December 1970 by concentration category for the 296 products . . . [shows that] the average *increase* for products with concentration ratios of 50 percent and over (5.9 percent) was nearly as great as the *decrease* for products with ratios of under 25 percent (−6.1 percent). Those in the intermediate group (for example, with ratios of from 25 to 49 percent) registered an intermediate change, declining −1.0 percent. . . . Obviously, the concentrated industries were more successful in translating higher costs (and perhaps other factors) into higher prices.

In the *Frankfurter Rundschau* (March 6, 1976) Herbert Shui summarized his study of the most recent recession in Germany:

> Industries in which a few big firms have a large share of the sales increased their prices significantly more in 1974–1975 than industries in which the largest firms do not have any above-average share of the market. The mirror image of the foregoing is that production declines in the highly concentrated industrial branches (those with the highest rates of inflation in the recession) significantly more than in the industrial sectors with only little concentration.

And writing on Argentina, Victor Testa has observed, in his *Aspectus económicos de la coyuntura actual, 1973–1975:*

> Full employment contributed to the ability of many groups to obtain additional increases in wages and salaries through their own efforts, and it contributed to spurring on the labor union militancy that was born out of the political process of these recent years. At the same time, without doubt this position of force of the working class drives the bourgeoisie to renew the inflationary process in order to recuperate their profit levels through price rises. Inflation as an answer to salary increases was a clearly applied policy in France in 1968, in Italy in 1969, and in Chile in 1970–1973, and it could not but turn up also in Argentina. What makes Argentina resemble France more than Chile is that the wage increases were obtained through worker action and not through official policy; what is similar in the three cases is that the answer of the bourgeoisie is the rise in prices and the inflation, which transfers the bid for income from the factory interior to the general economic front.

Roger Bratenstein writes:

> It seems remarkable that none of the [11 developed] countries with a steady uptrend of the national product in the review period . . . suffered from prolonged severe inflation. In contrast, the countries which experienced large price increases (Argentina, Bolivia, Brazil, Chile, Uruguay) were without exception hit by severe setbacks.[21]

Remarkable indeed—that he supposes setbacks in growth to be caused by inflation and steady uptrends to be possible only where inflation is absent. His correct correlation is not remarkable at all, because the "setbacks" in growth he registers are associated with recessionary declines in the rate of profit to which capital and its dutiful governments (even in Allende's 1970–1973 Chile) respond by increasing prices—and political repression.

But the "surest cure for inflation is a severe recession," as Royal Little, a living member of *Fortune's* Business Hall of Fame and founder of Textron Industries, recently observed.[22] Insofar as the threat to profits—which capital tries to recuperate by raising prices—was due in part to an increase in the wages of labor, the surest cure is a recession. However, it invariably needs a long recession, since wages usually lag behind the turn in the cycle (and the real wage rate, though not total wage payments, go up at the very beginning of a recession unless it is coupled with substantial inflation). Thus, after the long Kennedy–Johnson boom in the United States, capital demanded a recessionary attack on wages. President Nixon's administrator of the wage freeze, Arnold Weber, admitted that business "had been leaning" on the administration "to do something about wages. . . . The idea of the freeze and Phase II was to zap labor and we did."[23] More particularly, Nixon replaced the $12 billion budget surplus in 1967 by a $12 billion budget deficit in 1969, cutting welfare expenditures as part of the deliberate Nixon-Moynihan policy of dismantling the Kennedy New Frontier and the Johnson Great Society welfare programs. There seems little doubt that the 1969–1970 US recession was in large part deliberately induced by Nixon, though at that time he did not have the courage to persist with it long enough for it to do its job of reducing wages and disciplining labor and foreign competitors. Thus he re-sorted to the New Economic Policy of August 15, 1971, and the severe international depression that capital required was delayed until 1973–1975.

Deliberate recession as official Labour government strategy was also evident in the recent recession in Britain, where the *Financial Times* (February 25, 1975 and April 16, 1975) observed:

> The crux of the matter is simply this—that unemployment is rising quite fast . . . and that [Chancellor of the Exchequer] Mr.

Healey's commitment to offset excessive wage increases with restrictions on demand would tend to make it rise still faster. . . . The Chancellor has chosen to introduce a mildly deflationary budget. . . . It will be said—and not altogether without justification in view of Labour's resistance to direct controls over wage rates—that the Government has lost faith in the efficacy of the social contract and is relying instead on high unemployment to keep wage claims down to a reasonable level. The fact that Mr. Healey expressly and absolutely rejects the use of "mass unemployment" as an instrument of policy may well seem to those on the left of him to be no more than semantic quibbling.

Perhaps it is a bit more than quibbling, however, since Healey no doubt also kept in mind the warning of Trade Union Congress (TUC) General Secretary Len Murray (*Financial Times,* January 22, 1975) that "high unemployment would kill the social contract and with it the TUC's ability to secure a measure of voluntary wage restraint." On the other hand, as the *Economist* (September 21, 1974 and December 28, 1974) notes with satisfaction, strikes are correlated inversely with unemployment—as unemployment increases by 1 percent, strikes decline by 8 percent—but are positively correlated with wage declines, though controlled income policies can apparently break up this correlation. According to the *Economist* (September 21, 1974), "It is a popular misconception that wage controls produce more strikes. The reverse is usually true." Wage controls and incomes policy, the *Economist* points out, have in the United States and Britain resulted in *fewer* strikes. But of course, as Murray points out, for that the social contract must be preserved. If it is not, or if the bourgeoisie loses faith in its efficacy, the alternative is a policy of deliberate recession and unemployment.

Reviewing recent macroeconomic policy in several industrial capitalist countries, Oscar Braun wrote:

This deliberate policy of recession has sometimes been made explicit. In November 1974, the Chancellor of the Exchequer in Great Britain declared: "If wages rise beyond the limits set by the TUC, the government will be compelled to take offsetting steps to curtail demand. And the effects . . . are *bound to lead to unemployment."* In other words, if the workers ask for higher wages, the government shall take care to leave them without jobs. . . . The policy of "deliberate recession" was not exclusively British: it was worldwide. In the United States "the severity of the current recession can to a large extent be attributed to restrictive monetary and fiscal policies." In France, "by autumn the government's mid-year anti-inflationary measures—combined with the worsening international economic climate—rapidly reduced the pace of expansion." In Germany, "economic policy . . . last year singlemindedly focused on economic restraint." In Italy, "industrial production fell back dramatically largely because of the drastic measures taken to correct the high balance of payments and to slow down the inflation rate." In Japan, "the credit restrictions which were introduced at the end of 1973 . . . contributed significantly to the subsequent fall in output."

The international organizations, at the service of capital, support policies of deliberate recession no less enthusiastically: "More Jobless and Cutback in Growth Urged in IMF Report as Inflation Remedy" reads a headline in the London *Times* (September 16, 1974). In December 1975, at the beginning of the recovery, the OECD *Economic Outlook* (pp. 5,7) reported approvingly:

> A rather moderate recovery . . . might not be an unwelcome prospect for the countries concerned. . . . They cannot ignore the continuing high rate of inflation and the risk of giving it a new boost. . . . Policies appear more cautious than during previous recovery periods with governments determined to avoid repeating the mistakes of the 1972–1973 phase of excessive demand.

This "not unwelcome moderation of recovery" was taking place in countries which at that time still had around 1 million unemployed—except in the United States, which had about 8 million. Six months later, at the time of writing, the *Frankfurter Rundschau* (July 13, 1976)— reports under the subtitle "Weakening of Expansion Is Supposed to Avoid Overheating"—that the economic minister of the Bundesrepublik Germany, Hans Friedrichs, has observed "a certain weakening in the tempo of expansion after the starting phase, but that this development is in total accord with the growth strategy of [his] Ministry, which seeks to avoid early overheating." Meanwhile, unemployment exceeded 700,000 (and has risen to 1 million since then), not counting the "guest workers" who have returned to their countries of origin.

Still more ominous evidence of the contemporary policy of deliberate unemployment has come to light since mid-1976. As representative samples, I note the following two. In July 1976 the OECD published a *Special Supplement: A Growth Scenario to 1980,* which it took great care to introduce by saying:

> The figures shown, though they are based in part on national work on medium-term prospects and problems, should in no way be interpreted as representing either national or OECD Secretariat estimates of most likely developments over the coming four years. The aim of this exercise, as indicated by its title, is simply to present an internationally consistent set of figures illustrating one of a range of possible outcomes.

Nonetheless, the well-informed *Le Monde* (July 29, 1976) discussed this publication in an editorial entitled "The Dangerous Scenario of the OECD" and observed that:

> All these precautions are not enough to remove from this work its highly political character. It is [this document] which served as the basis of the discussion in the meeting of the ministers of the 24 member countries of the organization . . . on June 21 and 22 in Paris. After this conference a declaration was adopted.

This unusual attention and care by the OECD itself is merited because, as the document itself says (pp. 126–128):

> It is, rather, one possible scenario designed to pinpoint the difficulties and problems likely to be encountered in the formation of economic policy over these years. This scenario . . . identifies a number of *unwelcome features* which will be of major concern over the period, namely rates of inflation and unemployment notably higher than in the 1960s, and *significant divergences in economic performance between Member countries* which could run the risk of becoming self-perpetuating. . . . Under this scenario, output would, on average, grow from 1975 to 1980 by some 5½ percent per annum. . . . The period

from 1973 to 1980 is in many respects a more appropriate interval for considering the underlying trend . . . at just under 4 percent per annum. . . . For a number of countries unemployment is likely to remain a serious issue over the years to come. . . . The same is, of course, true for inflation. . . . There is indeed a danger that the range of developments in individual countries could be wider than that shown in the scenario. It would, of course, be tempting to consider a more favorable scenario in which full employment of resources was achieved more rapidly without a serious resurgence of inflation and with less divergence in performance between countries. Unfortunately, there are few grounds for believing that this is a realistic alternative unless economic policies prove much more effective than in the past. Attempts to pursue a significantly faster growth rate would almost certainly lead the world back into the 1973–1975 experiences of inflation followed by recession. The central problem for policy common to all countries is the rate of inflation . . . [not the unemployment that remains since 1973–1975!] . . . a relatively moderate recovery . . . would be preferable to a sharp upturn.

The document continues (pp. 134–138):

Analysis of the present scenario permits identification of some of the key policy problems that might arise. . . . A special effort will have to be made in many countries to restrain the medium-term growth rate of consumption, both private and public, in order to meet two main demand requirements in the period covered by the projections. These are (i) an increase in the share of investment in output. . . . (ii) An increased share of exports. . . . The present projections [no longer single "scenarios"!] envisage implicitly a sizeable shift in income distribution from the OECD to the OPEC area in the international sphere and from labor to capital at home. This is, of course, the counterpart to the shifts in resource allocation toward exports and investment. . . . In the first instance a revival of investment demand depends on strengthened confidence in the likelihood of a sustained rise in sales and profits. In the longer run, some action may be necessary to ensure that the revival of business investment is not choked off for lack of profit or of equity capital. . . . There seems, however, to be, at least in some countries, a strong apprehension that insufficient profitability and/or highly geared financing of these investment flows may jeopardize their achievement. . . . This implies a reduction in the growth rates of real wages and hence consumption of the population of the area as a whole, relative to the growth of output . . . at least over the medium-term. . . . A slowdown in public expenditure is planned in a number of countries.

No wonder the OECD exercises the cautions of its introductory disclaimers, if this is the scenario of the problems to be encountered in the formation of economic policy over these years.

The OECD clarifies the issue further in its next *Economic Outlook,* published in December 1976 (pp. 5–6):

> The fact that the recovery seems to have tapered off significantly and so soon in the countries where strong home demand would be appropriate, has been regarded by some observers as a mark of failure. . . . Such judgment, with its undertones of pessimism for the future, seems highly questionable. It would be truer to say that policies have produced very largely what their authors expected of them. . . . When it came to reflationary action in 1975, governments were intentionally cautious in handing out fiscal stimulus, despite the existence of large slack. . . . Governments were, in most cases, similarly cautious in the monetary policy that accommodated this recovery as it developed because the lessons of the previous revival phase were plain to see. Under these circumstances it was not surprising that, as the effects of fiscal stimulus wore off and the change in the inventory cycle worked itself through, recovery slackened. . . . Given what was at stake, it can be considered a mark of success, not failure. . . . Very quick return to full employment and capacity use is considered a fruitless aim.

A still more revealing sample of deliberate unemployment policy is the major article by Sanford Rose in *Fortune* (September 1976) entitled "We've Learned How to Lick Inflation." The editors introduce the article as follows: "This article is the first in a *Fortune* series, 'An Agenda for the New Administration.'. . . To a considerable extent the articles in the series will be prescriptive." This article was published at a time when US unemployment had just risen from its post-1974 minimum "low" of 7.3 percent, in May 1976, to 7.8 percent in September, and would continue to rise to 8.1 percent in November. It reads in part (pp. 100–106):

Yet there is every reason to believe that an unremitting war on inflation should be our major national priority. . . . In 1969 it was generally believed at the Council of Economic Advisors that all we needed to lick inflation was a bit of old-fashioned medicine: a recession. We got a recession in 1970 and another in 1974–1975, but prices kept moving up. Many economists became discouraged. . . . The rate of inflation is roughly equal to the increase in earnings less the increase in productivity. . . . Thus, if we wish to push the basic inflation rate down . . . the only sure way to achieve this is to maintain a greater degree of slackness in the labor market than we have had during most of the last ten years. It is clear that once the unemployment rate falls below a certain point, it becomes increasingly difficult, if not impossible, to control inflation. But for many years, economists thought that this point was around 4 percent—a figure that got to be called the "full employment" rate of unemployment. Now it turns out that 4 percent is far too low. *In fact, it has been too low for the past 28 years.* According to an analysis done by MIT's Professor Robert Hall, one of our leading labor-market economists, the sustainable rate of unemployment—the rate below which inflation starts accelerating—was around 5 percent as far back as 1948 and has gradually risen to between 5.5 and 6 percent in the last few years. . . . Calculations made by Franco Modigliani, also of MIT, more or less confirm Hall's findings.

The sustainable or "natural" rate of unemployment, as it is now called, is reached when there is an approximate balance between the supply of and demand for highly productive workers (e.g., prime-age males): at this point, there would be an excess supply of less productive workers (i.e., teenagers). When the unemployment rate is pushed below its natural levels by over-expansive monetary and fiscal policies . . . wages are bid up to much higher levels. . . . From 1951 to 1953 . . . unemployment fell well below its natural rate. . . . From 1964 to 1970, the unemployment rate again fell below the natural rate, to 4.9 percent, the rise in compensation escalated to 7.8 percent. These figures make it clear that unemployment must remain at much higher levels than conventional political rhetoric demands. . . . Ideally the whole operation should be so timed that . . . the unemployment rate falls to between 5.5 and 6 percent. . . . However, it would be imprudent to aim for this ideal situation. In practice, it is next to impossible for the government to accomplish any such fine-tuning. It would be better to err on the side of conservatism, and to stop nudging down the unemployment rate when it gets close to 6 percent. If we adopted this posture, the rate of increase in hourly earnings would continue falling. There is no doubt that the rate has been pushed down by the high unemployment rates of the last couple of years.

In a box accompanying this article, *Fortune* also reports "The Good News from Professor Wachter":

> Among economists who specialize in the problems of wage inflation, one of the most optimistic these days is Michael Wachter, that young man (he is 33) at the right. Wachter, a professor at the University of Pennsylvania, has done some calculations indicating that the trade-off between wage increases and unemployment has recently become much more favorable, i.e., a given degree of unemployment has a greater effect in holding down the rate of wage gains. . . . The slack labor markets prevailing since late 1974 have reduced labor's ability to command any such wage rise. In effect, the entire Phillips curve has been pushed "southwest." . . . As unemployment continues falling, we could lose some of this benefit.

But anxiety was unnecessary since unemployment was rising at that time, and has since gone up further! Thus *Fortune* proudly gives its account of how economists on the right are busily engaged in revising the "natural" laws of "natural" unemployment to suit the needs of business for a pseudoscientific ideological figleaf to cover their naked political prescriptions "for the new administration." Lawrence Klein, who is emerging as Jimmy Carter's principal economic advisor, has recently suggested that a 7 percent inflation rate in 1977 should not disturb us—even though in August 1976 (no doubt mistakenly!) he still regarded anything over 4 percent unemployment as real unemployment, which he wanted to eliminate more than inflation.

At the time of the publication of the *Fortune* article, Jimmy Carter was campaigning for the presidency with the conventional political rhetoric of fighting unemployment. In September, however, according to a *New York Times* (September 5,

1976) headline, "Carter Shifts His Emphasis on US Spending, Stresses Inflation Curbs, Balanced Budget," saying that he would delay the start of "costly programs" if elected president, "in what appeared to be a distinct shift of political emphasis." In later statements, particularly since the election when official unemployment was over 7 percent, Carter announced the appointment of a "conservative" as director of the Office of the Budget. Now (*U.S. News & World Report,* December 13, 1976) he aims to bring the growth rate up from 4 to 6 percent and perhaps to cut the rate of unemployment to 4 percent by the end of this four-year term and to regard this as "a notable achievement" in meeting his goal of bringing unemployment down 1.5 points in 1977, from 7.9 percent to 6.4 percent! But by November the official rate of unemployment had jumped to 8.1 percent and the *New York Times* reported in an editorial that "some economists argue that 8 percent unemployment is now 'normal,' or only slightly above an acceptable rate" (*International Herald Tribune,* November 10, 1976). As the cited article in *Fortune* correctly noted, "Fashions in economic thought change with remarkable suddenness"—especially when the cyclical imperatives of capital's economic interests and its political executors suddenly require a new economic ideology. Little wonder that in face of the reality of massive unemployment and this ideological offensive designed to make it "natural," "a large majority—66 percent—feel that full employment in the United States is no longer a realistic goal." Only somewhat less explicable is that in assigning blame and responsibility for this unemployment, according to the same survey and source, 69 percent blame the government, 65 percent blame the labor unions, and 38 percent say business must take some responsibility (*U.S. News & World Report,* September 13, 1976).

In the meantime British Prime Minister James Callaghan addressed a Labour Party conference on September 28, 1976, and told his listeners:

> We used to think that you could just spend your way out of a recession and increase employment by cutting taxes and boosting government spending. I tell you, in all candor, that the

option no longer exists, and that insofar as it ever did exist, it only worked by injecting bigger doses of inflation into the economy, followed by higher levels of unemployment as the next step. That is the history of the past twenty years. (*Newsweek,* December 6, 1976)

Thus in the mother country of Keynes and Keynesianism,

Britain's Labour government today abandoned thirty years of Keynesian policy and announced a stiff £1.9 billion ($3.4 billion) deflationary package at a time of high and rising unemployment. . . . The decision on such a tough set of measures is seen here as a triumph for US Treasury Secretary William Simon and conservative international financiers. In public and private, they have been warning Mr. Healey that he could expect no more help for the ailing pound unless he tightened Britain's belt. . . . Mr. Healey and Mr. Callaghan have turned this doctrine [conventional Keynesian economics] on its head. . . . The opposition Conservatives have been calling for just such measures and so applauded Mr. Healey today. (*International Herald Tribune,* July 23, 1976)

To make sure that Callaghan and Healey keep up the good work and have the political courage to overcome resistance within the Labour Party and trade union movement, the IMF is keeping tabs on them and threatening to withhold its lifesaving $3.9 billion loan:

Economic advisors to major Swiss banks say Britain needs . . . the asked-for loan of $3.9 billion from the International Monetary Fund, and the requirement that a stable Labour government stay at the helm, because it alone can pursue the conservative policies that are necessary to prop up the economy. . . . What is needed is a "solid conservative government," says Union Bank of Switzerland economist Mr. Wyler. He chuckles and adds: "And Labour right now are the better chance of providing that." (*International Herald Tribune,* November 13–14, 1976)

In France, in the meantime, the new professional economist Prime Minister Raymond Barre proposed an austerity plan that, according to an estimate in *Le Monde,* would cost French workers between 5 percent and 15 percent of their income, depending upon the scale of its implementation. No wonder that the workers paralyzed the country in a general strike. In Italy, on the other hand, the Christian Democrats are already applying Andreotti's austerity program, with the support of the Communist Party. Other such austerity programs were being implemented, on the basis of various different political coalitions, in late 1976 in European countries as varied as Portugal, Spain, Ireland, Denmark, Greece, Turkey, and Finland. Little wonder then that some

> Wall Street analysts have begun focusing on something more basic than a pause or a lull. . . . One says, "The growth of most European economies during 1977 will be, at best, slightly worse than in 1976 and, at worst, nearly disastrous." The crux of both analyses is the uncertain impact on the world's economy of deflationary policies being undertaken by several countries. These policies are aimed at reducing, rather than spurring, total domestic demand. . . . "Considering that these deflationary measures have been adopted in a climate of high unemployment and slowing economic growth, one must concede they are at least well-intentioned," he says. But he believes it is still questionable whether they can achieve intended results without a severe retrenchment in employment, or that the political climate abroad is strong enough to permit their implementation. (*International Herald Tribune,* November 4, 1976)

What little doubt remains that national governments' macroeconomic policy in industrialized—let alone underdeveloped—countries is a class-based policy to use state power in the interests of the capitalist class in accord with the long-, middle-, and short-run exigencies of the necessarily uneven process of accumulation through the exploitation of labor should be finally dispelled by recent events. The claim that national macroeconomic policy is designed to, and can, produce healthy, progressive growth on a high plane for the people at large, is nothing but the ruling capitalist class's ideological myth.

Even if this ideological myth were or could be true—which it is not and cannot be—on the national plane, it has absolutely no efficacy at all on an international plane. In an interview given to *Time* (May 10, 1976) German Chancellor and ex-

Minister of Finance Helmut Schmidt warned, "Everybody has to bear in mind that it is the world's economy that must be pulled out of the mess, and not just one's own national economy. This holds true to some degree even for the United States." The "economic summits" at Rambouillet Castle in France in 1975 and in Puerto Rico in 1976 testify to high-level political concern for—and at the same time the inability to deal with—the problem of stabilizing and guiding the international economy through national state policies. In an interview with *Business Week* (January 13, 1975) after the first of these summits, Henry Kissinger admitted that "one interesting feature of our recent discussions with both the Europeans and the Japanese has been the emphasis on the need for economic coordination. . . . How you, in fact, coordinate policies is yet an unresolved problem."

The renowned economist Gottfried Haberler has observed the obvious: "Inflation is an international phenomenon, but it can be stopped only by national policies. The main responsibility clearly lies with the largest countries. . . . Small countries have little choice."[24] Less obvious but no less true is his observation that "the world is no longer on the dollar standard . . . but it is still true that US inflation will have an inflationary influence in other parts of the world. Moreover, the United States is capable of 'exporting' inflation to some countries even if it has no inflation . . . at home. That is to say, world inflation was made in the United States."[25] That is precisely what the United States did during the deficit-financed, Eurodollar-generating war against Vietnam: keeping inflation under a measure of control at home but exporting it abroad, and letting the devil take the hindmost. From a different point of view, Sweezy and Magdoff wrote in 1970:

> Since the Americanization of the Vietnam War, a robust export surplus of approximately $6 billion in 1964 largely disappeared by 1969. The result has of course been a drastic weakening of the US balance-of-payments position: on an international scale the United States is now living far beyond its means. . . . Up to now the other capitalist countries have been willing to accept more and more US dollars on the implicit

assumption that they are a form of IOU which can eventually be cashed in. . . . The question . . . is how long this can go on. . . . But one thing does seem sure: the piling up of IOU's cannot go on forever. There must come a time, sooner or later, when the creditors will say "No more!" and begin to try to collect on what they already have. And that would mean the breakdown of the present international monetary system, with consequences perhaps even more profound and widespread than those which followed the breakdown of the international monetary system in 1931.[26]

Soon after this, on August 15, 1971, the United States stopped officially converting the dollar into gold: the dollar was twice devalued, the major currencies floated against each other, after several speculative currency crises had made it impossible to maintain pegged rates, and the whole international monetary system built up at Bretton Woods at the end of the war crumbled. Despite repeated attempts to patch things up, so far all the king's men have not been able to put Humpty Dumpty together again.

A repeat of the 1931 monetary breakdown is still possible, and the recurrence, albeit in different forms, of the 1929 (in many respects really 1928 or even 1927) to 1933 (or really 1940) depression is also possible, if not probable. The problem of how, if at all, to coordinate national state macroeconomic policies is as unresolved now as it was then.

Representing the desire of US imperialism to dominate its European and Japanese rivals, not to mention the Third World, Charles Kindleberger, in a recent book on the Great Depression, argued that it had not been possible to prevent the slump because there existed no *one* dominant economic power at the time: Britain had already declined and the United States was not yet willing or able to assert itself sufficiently.[27] Without accompanying Kindleberger so far as to agree that a super-imperialist power can, or should, exist or that it could have prevented the last depression and could prevent any future one, I agree that interimperialist rivalries, then and now, render the coordination or the success of national macroeconomic stabilization policies well-nigh impossible when put to the test

of severe depressive strain. For such depressions convert all
national macroeconomic policies into beggar-my-neighbor
policies to export national production and unemployment.
Thus, shortly before the 1929 crash the Young Plan for German
war reparations was signed, despite German complaints that it
was then unable to pay the reparations assigned it. Indeed,
formal acceptance of the Young Plan did not come until
January 1930, *after* the crash, thus aggravating the economic
depressionary and politically explosive trends by trying to
export problems from one country to the next. Hoover did not
propose a moratorium on German reparations until June 20,
1931, after it had become clear not only that Germany could
not pay but that the attempt to force it to do so burdened the
world capitalist economy as a whole; and even then acceptance
of the moratorium was delayed by France's recalcitrance. In
June 1930, the US Congress passed the highly protective
Hawley-Smoot Tariff, in an attempt to export the burden of
the crisis. In the meantime financial crisis rocked Austria,
Germany, and Britain, which suddenly abandoned the hal-
lowed gold standard in September 1931, only a few weeks
after the high-level Macmillan Commission (including Keynes
as a leading member) had announced that Britain should not and
would not take this drastic step. This was followed by twenty-
five other countries also abandoning the gold standard to save
their own macroeconomic policies as far as circumstances still
allowed, which was not far. The economic "summit" of the time
was the World Economic and Monetary Conference, which
after several postponements finally met in London in June and
July 1933. By that time Hitler and Roosevelt had come to
office, and it was the latter who totally wrecked the conference
and thereby the last hope of any coordination, by his intransi-
gence in trying to collect foreign-owed debts and by pursuing
unilateral monetary and fiscal policies and then suddenly and
unexpectedly refusing to accept the resolution agreeing on
cooperative currency stabilization which the US delegation
had helped draft and which had earlier been proposed by
Roosevelt himself. President Nixon's New Economic Policy
and his abandonment of gold on August 15, 1971, his blackmail
of allies, especially Japan—which suffered the most from the

"Nixon shock" of the 10 percent surtax—shows that nothing has improved in forty years. This hardly represents a promise of healthy, progressive macroeconomic policy for the next crisis.

We may agree with Schmidt's observation at the National Press Club in Washington (as reported in *Frankfurter Rundschau,* July 17, 1976) that the time of self-sufficient national economies is forever past—though of course it was already "past" in the sixteenth century, before the national state was even born. We must also agree with Fred Block:

> The point is simple: the greater the openness of the world economy, the greater the extent of international economic interdependence and the greater the need for institutions to manage the international economy in the same way central banks and national governments manage domestic economies [God forbid!]. The problem, of course, is how one establishes such an international institutional structure in a world of competing nation states. Three basic solutions to the problem exist: the exercise of this coordinating and managing role by one dominant and responsible power; the development of supranational institutions to which national governments cede important elements of economic sovereignty; and the development of an effective joint partnership among a number of major nations that would coordinate the world economy in their common interest. The international monetary system has worked best in those periods when one nation had the economic and political power to assure general acceptance of a code of international economic bahavior and could provide by itself adequate quantities of international credit and liquidity. But the continuing US balance of payments deficits indicate that the US no longer has the absolute economic superiority to fulfill that coordinating role. And if the US lacks that power, certainly no other country or region can even pretend that it could play that role. This leaves only the second or third solutions as possible means toward international economic coordination today. . . . Governments would be extremely reluctant to turn over to an international agency the right to defend or improve their country's international position. . . . Joint management would most likely involve significant shifts in US (and other countries') foreign and domestic policies.[28]

This they would be least likely to undertake, particularly in times of crisis.

7. EQUATING ECONOMIC FORECASTING WITH ASTROLOGY IS AN INSULT— TO ASTROLOGERS

A public opinion poll showed that Americans ranked the forecasting ability of economists just about on a par with that of astrologers.

—*Fortune,* January 1976

"The Administration's statements had been so vague that they had the character of a Greek oracle," complains one New York banker. "People were becoming cynical about what it really had in mind."

—*Business Week,* January 16, 1978

Lies, damn'd lies and forecasts.

—*Financial Times,* December 19, 1978

Whenever I get worried about the economy, I go up to the top of the mountain to see the Great Exalted Economist. "Blessed Guru, what is the answer?" "We must hold our hand firmly on the rudder until the storm blows over, keeping all options open even if it means tightening our belts." "I knew you would have the answer, Exalted One," I said with tears in my eyes. He turned to go into his cave. . . . The last words he said to me were, "Then again, I could be wrong."

—Art Buchwald, *International Herald Tribune,* June 8, 1978

Recent economic forecasting is on a par with astrology and the oracle of Delphi is tending to accentuate the positive and eliminate the negative while—apparently intentionally—letting everyone make their own interpretations of the forecasts in accordance with their interests and experience. If there is any

This essay was first published in *Contemporary Crises,* vol. 4, no. 1, 1980.

other method in the forecasters' madness, it is more obscure than the proverbial clouded crystal ball and certainly more irresponsible than that of the astrologers, who at least contradict themselves less. Insofar as they can be checked at all, and despite their vagueness, mutual contradictions, and bandwagon effects, the worth of the predictions' accuracy is nil, as we have shown elsewhere.

Surveying below the economic forecasts and statements of high government officials, prestigious economic and political research institutions, leading business figures and economists, econometric forecasting organizations, opinion surveys, and last but not least the business and daily press, we find over the course of 1977 the most total confusion, combining ignorance, whitewashing, contradictory statements, arbitrary selection and tendentious interpretation of statements, events, and data, as well as just plain irresponsibility in the most "responsible" organs of economic prediction. Equating these "responsible" sources with astrology is an insult indeed—to astrologers.

Though our oracles, often apparently intentionally, are sometimes ambiguous, we may classify them into "bad news" and "good news"—and see how one is interpreted as the other and how the oracles contradict each other, and even themselves, at nearly the same time and place. (Unless otherwise noted, all citations are from headlines or quotations in the *International Herald Tribune* in 1977, modified only to identify the person quoted. Michael Blumenthal was US secretary of the treasury, Charles Schultze was chairman of the Council of Economic Advisors, and Bert Lance was past director of the Office of the Budget.)

Bad News	*Good News*
BLUMENTHAL SAYS UPTURN WON'T LAST. SCHULTZE SEEMS TO DISAGREE (March 3)	BLUMENTHAL: AHEAD AT LEAST 3 YEARS OF PROSPERITY (*U.S. News & World Report,* April 4)
BLUMENTHAL ADMITS US IN SLOWDOWN. BUT WE ARE NOT CONCERNED IT IS A REAL RECESSION (September 23)	US ECONOMIC GROWTH SEEN GOOD THROUGH '78—CHARLES SCHULTZE (September 14)

Bad News	Good News
BLUMENTHAL SAYS RECOVERY AT STANDSTILL	SCHULTZE SAYS UPTURN WILL CONTINUE (September 14)
WASHINGTON FORECASTS SURPRISINGLY DARK—OFFICE OF THE BUDGET (May 2)	CARTER'S BUDGET CHIEF ON US ECONOMY: LANCE "PLEASED BUT NOT SATISFIED" (July 11)
DOUBTS PERSIST ABOUT STRENGTH OF RECOVERY. ONLY 20% SURVEYED: "GOOD"—CONFERENCE BOARD SURVEY (March 28)	US GROWTH SEEN BALANCED, HEALTHY—CONFERENCE BOARD (June 20)
MODEST EXPANSION—CONFERENCE BOARD ECONOMIC FORUM (August 12)	
ONLY SMALL PROFIT GAINS SEEN FOR US FIRMS (May 3) WALL STREET FIRM CUTS PROFIT OUTLOOK (June 29)	US PROFITS SURPASS FORECASTS (April 30)
INVESTMENT STRENGTH STILL MISSING (April 29)	ANALYSTS SEE RAPID GROWTH IN '77 (April 4)
WASHINGTON MOVES DIM BUSINESS OPTIMISM (May 16)	CONFIDENCE WILL WARM UP (*Fortune*, March)
US HEADING FOR RECESSION IN '78, SOME ECONOMISTS SAY. CHASE ECONOMETRIC—GNP GROWTH ZERO FIRST HALF '78 (September 9)	EVEN BETTER TIMES COMING AS TOP BUSINESS ANALYSTS SEE IT FOR 1977 AND BEYOND (*U.S. News & World Report*, April 8)
CHASE ECONOMETRIC EXPECTS REAL GROWTH 1.6% DURING 1978 (September 2)	FOR US ECONOMY: A SUNNY MIDYEAR OUTLOOK (*U.S. News & World Report*, July 4) ONLY FEAR OF INFLATION MARS OPTIMISTIC MOOD (May 9)

Bad News	*Good News*
SLOW US GROWTH SEEN OVER NEXT YEARS—SLOW TO ABOUT 4.3% IN 1978.—LAWRENCE KLEIN, WHARTON ECONOMETRIC FORECASTING (September 21)	CONFIDENCE ON EXPANSION IN US—EXECUTIVES EXPECT ECONOMIC GROWTH TO CONTINUE (September 17/18)
US GROWTH SEEN SLOWING IN '78— NATIONAL ASSOCIATION OF BUSINESS ECONOMISTS (October 11)	
SLOWER US GROWTH PREDICTED— CONFERENCE BOARD FORUM (November 29)	US ECONOMIC SCENE: MIDWEST BUSINESS OUTLOOK REFLECTS OPTIMISM (December 5)
US ECONOMIC SCENE: PESSIMISM CONTINUES TO DARKEN OUTLOOK (October 17)	BLUMENTHAL SAYS US MAY BOOST ECONOMY IN '78 (November 2)
US BUSINESS CONFIDENCE HAS CRACKED. THE SURVEYS SAY SO (November 19)	

European and other leaders, institutions, and "responsible" sources of economic forecasts seem, on balance, to be more pessimistic than their US colleagues, though they are no less free of wishful thinking (or at least talking), sudden changes, bandwagon effects, and outright contradictions, as the following few selected announcements and pronouncements suggest. (The source here is also the *International Herald Tribune* in 1977, unless otherwise noted. Helmut Schmidt was prime minister of West Germany and Hans Friedrichs was minister of economics.)

Bad News	*Good News*
We are approaching a phase similar to the World Depression, in which the international division of labor could be disturbed—indeed, deeply destroyed—and this phase may last not twelve months	SCHMIDT MINIMIZES MAIN PROBLEMS: "I DO NOT SEE ANY KIND OF CRISIS AT ALL" (March 21, 1977)

Bad News	Good News
but several years. . . . We are today on the high road thereto. (Helmut Schmidt, *Die Zeit,* February 15, 1974)	
FRIEDRICHS' PROPHETS SEE BLACK IN FUTURE: UNEMPLOYMENT, INFLATION, PROTECTIONISM (*Frankfurter Rundschau,* September 20)	FRIEDRICHS PREDICTS REAL GROWTH OF 9 TO 10 PERCENT FOR 1977 (*Frankfurter Rundschau,* March 2)
NEW WEST GERMAN DATA CONFIRM POOR OUTLOOK (September 2)	Herbert Giersch, president of the Institute of World Economy in Kiel and formerly chief economic advisor to the West German government, predicted Europe's recovery probably vigorous in 1977 (*U.S. News & World Report,* July 19, 1976)
BUNDESBANK SAYS RECOVERY AT A STANDSTILL. LAGGING EXPORTS, LOW INVESTMENT CITED (September 9)	
EEC PESSIMISTIC ON FIRM RECOVERY (March 11)	GERMAN MANUFACTURING INDUSTRY EXPECTS 11 PERCENT INCREASE IN SALES IN 1977, ACCORDING TO ECONOMIC RESEARCH INSTITUTE SURVEY (*Frankfurter Rundschau,* March 12)
OECD REVISES FORECASTS DOWN. OUTLOOK GLOOMY (November 11)	
OECD STAKES LOWER SIGHTS ON '78 GOALS (November 23)	
GLOBAL ECONOMY CALLED "UNSATISFACTORY" BY IMF. OUTLOOK GLOOMY (September 12)	
UNCTAD WARNS OF NEW SLUMP NEXT YEAR (August 18)	
BRITISH REPORT MORE PESSIMISTIC. LOW GROWTH PREDICTED FOR WORLD ECONOMY (November 30)	

This regrettable, if not disgraceful, jumble of "optimistic" and "pessimistic" forecasts and predictions is appropriately complemented by statements that are literally impossible to classify, unless it is simultaneously under the categories "head in the sand" and "head in the clouds":

BLUMENTHAL REASSURES BUSINESSMEN ON CARTER

Mr. Blumenthal acknowledged the "troubling paradox" of "on the one hand, good economic recovery in 1977 and reasonably good prospects for 1978 and, on the other, the lowest level of business confidence in a long time." (*International Herald Tribune,* October 21, 1977)

Part of the "paradox" might be resolved for Blumenthal if he acknowledged the disgraceful record of his own contradictory and irresponsible performance as US secretary of the treasury (as revealed in part in our first and last quotations above).

But the press is not to be outdone by the politicians, not even in its hard-nosed, feet-on-the-ground financial pages:

US ECONOMISTS SEE SLOWDOWN.
BUT THEY WERE WRONG BEFORE
(*International Herald Tribune,* July 7, 1977)

THE US ECONOMIC SCENE:
COMFORT IS FOUND IN THE IMPRECISION OF STATISTICS.
NEWS GOOD AND BAD

When consideration is given to the recent array of unsettling economic statistics, it becomes quite difficult for even the most rabid optimists to remain highly confident about fairly strong growth in the months immediately ahead. There is, however, one major comforting factor: the belief that much of the current data, whether negative or positive, may be somewhat misleading because of faulty seasonal adjustments or other problems. (*New York Times,* August 7, 1977)

Comforting indeed—especially when we consider the press reportage and interpretation of these data to boot!

While rabid optimists may take comfort in the misleading imprecision of the economic astrology, political soothsaying, and journalistic oracles cited above, more pedestrian realists may consider—and ordinary workers must suffer the implications and consequences of—the following problems that do not seem to be subject to seasonal adjustment (and are variously also reported in the press). The capitalist world suffered its most severe recession since the 1930s in the two years between mid-1973 (*before* the oil crisis!) and mid-1975, during which time world capitalist production and trade declined. Since then, there has been a cyclical "recovery" based on sales to consumers and exports, especially to the Middle East and the Soviet bloc. But despite this so-called recovery, *investment* has not recovered and at the end of 1977 still remains *below* its 1973 level; and all "predictions" forecast (in this case more accurately and responsibly) that investment will not increase substantially in the foreseeable future. Moreover, much of the investment to date has not been used to expand productive facilities, but to "rationalize" productive methods to eliminate jobs. During the recession, officially registered unemployment (which is widely acknowledged to be far less than true unemployment) in the Office of Economic Cooperation and Development (OECD) industrialized countries rose to 16 million, of which about 9 million was in the United States. During the recovery, unemployment in the United States has fallen back to about 7 million; but in Western Europe, Canada, Australia, and Japan, it has *risen* to about 10 million. Total registered OECD unemployment today is therefore about 17 million, or *more* than it was at the depth of the recession. For some categories—women, teenagers, and those who are racially and ethnically discriminated against, and particularly among those who combine two or even three of these handicaps—unemployment rates rise from 10 percent to 50 percent and more. And these unemployment rates have become structurally so chronic even at 1976–1977 "recovery" growth rates that there has been no possibility of eliminating or even halting the further growth of these rates, even with the most rabid optimistic projections. But the failure of investment to recover and expand, which already manifests itself in declining growth rates—and successive official downward "adjustments" of future growth-rate predictions—not to mention all prudent economic theory based on the historical experience of capitalist growth, portend the approach of another recession, possibly with a still greater decline in production and trade than in 1973–1975. The resulting decline of employment/increase of unemployment will not start from the lower "normal" unemployment before the last recession, but will be added on to the already existing high rate of unemployment.

8. WORLD CRISIS THEORY AND IDEOLOGY

Crisis does not mean the end. On the contrary, crisis refers to the critical time during which the end will be avoided through new adaptations; only if these fail does the end become unavoidable. The dictionary defines crisis as a "turning point, especially of disease. Moment of danger or suspense in politics, etc., as cabinet, financial. From Greek *krisis,* decision." The crisis is a period in which a diseased social, economic, and political body cannot live on as before and is obliged, on pain of death, to undergo transformations that will give it a new lease on life. Therefore, this period of crisis is a historical moment of danger and suspense during which the crucial decisions and transformations are made that will determine the future development of the system and its new social, economic, and political base.

The unsatisfactory recovery from the 1973–1975 recession has led to growing public realization that the new world crisis is not a locally or temporally restricted phenomenon that will soon pass. Political leaders and the press have drawn increasing parallels with the 1930s, though perhaps such comparisons are insufficient, in view of the development of fascism and war that were part and parcel of that crisis. Increasingly economic historians can draw analogies between the development of the present crisis and the period between the two world wars, as well as the crisis of a century ago, which was associated with the so-called great depression of 1873–1895. The latter crisis

This essay summarizes many of the findings in two recent books by the author, *Crisis: In the World Economy* and *Crisis: In the Third World,* published in 1980 and 1981, respectively, by Holmes & Meier in New York and Heinemann in London.

resulted in the rise of monopoly capitalism and imperialism, but also the end of Pax Britannica, as Britain began its decline from world leadership in the face of challenges from Germany and the United States. The present world crisis seems to be spelling the beginning of the end of Pax Americana and may hold untold other major readjustments in the international division of labor and world power in store for the future.

In the international capitalist economy accumulation on a world scale can no longer proceed as it did in the postwar era of expansion, until and unless unequal development and dependent accumulation are put on a new footing. Among the most important elements of the new, emerging international division of labor are the reintegration of the socialist economies into the world market, the transfer of certain world market industries both to them and to selected parts of the Third World, where wages are lower and labor discipline is higher, and the "rationalization" of industrial production in the West itself through investment in labor-saving technology, unemployment, and depressed wages. It was no accident that when trade among the industrial capitalist countries declined by nearly 15 percent in 1975, industrial exports to the socialist countries and the Third World increased sufficiently so that total world trade only declined by 5 percent. Profits from exports to and work done in the East and the South have continued to provide a significant safety net for business and government in the West since then, while the focus of stagnating investment has shifted from the creation of new production facilities to the rationalization of existing ones with excess capacity.

The concomitant social and political transformations that necessarily accompany this new international division of labor include militarism, war, East-West competition in the South, détente and a Washington-Peking-Tokyo axis with the East, technological rationalization and economic austerity policies based on the "national interest." While these tactics lack the erstwhile legitimation of a Red scare, there is nonetheless a new "defense gap"—reminiscent of the phony missile gap of the 1960s, but apparently without consideration of the subsequent credibility gap in the West. It is to be expected that all these economic, social, and political transformations pose serious challenges to existing policy and ideology.

The new political economic crisis throughout the world is also producing a crisis—or rather, crises—of ideology and theory, which cry out for alternative applications of social theory to political practice. In the "first world" of the industrialized, capitalist West (including Japan, Australia, and New Zealand), the deepest economic crisis in over a generation is reviving long forgotten memories of the Great Depression, if not yet of the two world wars themselves. The push of economic and political crisis in the "second world" of the East and the pull of the West in crisis are increasingly reintegrating the socialist economies in the changing capitalist international division of labor. Both of these crises, as well as the failure of two decades of development in the "third world," are imposing cheap labor and political oppression on the peoples in most of the countries of the South and raising their doubts about the value of national liberation and the prospects for socialism. The various parts of the world are increasingly integrated into a single economic system through the intervention of increasingly powerful and repressive states. Yet, paradoxically, a new wave of nationalism is threatening international relations between, and challenging authority within, national states all around the world. These real social crises in various parts of the world—or are they reflections of a crisis in a single world system?—are also producing crises in theory and ideology throughout the world.

The manifestly increasing—and increasingly manifest—inadequacy of partial theories to analyze this worldwide crisis cries out for alternative theory and ideology. The titles of many recent publications—*The Crisis of Democracy,* Report on the Governability of Democracies to the Trilateral Commission; *The Alternative,* by the East German Communist Rudolph Bahro; *The Limits to Growth* and *Reshaping the International Order,* by the Club of Rome—as well as the demand incited by the Third World countries of the United Nations for a New International Economic Order are some of the visible manifestations of crisis and the resulting search for new theoretical perspectives. Though all of these seek to predict and shape the future, not one of them draws on a historical perspective or views the past, present, and future as sequences in a single historical process. Moreover, with the notable exception of Bahro, these ideological efforts have been undertaken—sometimes very self-consciously—on behalf of the already ruling classes or dominant groups in the West and South.

Like previous major expansions, industrial expansion after World War II produced an excess of capital relative to the labor used (in Marxist terminology, an increase in the organic composition of capital), particularly in industry. Together with relative overinvestment in capital equipment in industry, there was relative underinvestment in productive capacity in the mining and agricultural sectors in most of the capitalist world. Not incidentally, this is substantially responsible for the oil and agricultural crises of the 1970s and perhaps the 1980s. Since the mid-1960s in the industrial economies the increase in the capital-labor ratio and productivity, as well as the associated increase in worker bargaining power and militancy, have led to a decline in the rate of profit, the rate of growth, and in some instances to an absolute reduction in the demand for industrial commodities, particularly capital or investment goods. The previous imbalance may now lead to a relative increase in the provision of raw materials and agricultural products. Additionally, productivity and production have grown at different rates in the major industrial capitalist economies. Until recently, productivity in Western Europe has grown at twice the US rate, and Japan's at four times the US rate.

One consequence of these developments has been the attempt to postpone, restrain, or—in some monopolized sectors—prevent the decline in the rate of profit and the restriction in the market through massive infusions of printed money and credit into the economy. This effort took its most spectacular form in the United States through the deficit financing of the war against Vietnam, which flooded the world with dollars. Secondly, competition increased, particularly among national sectors of capital from one country to another for the remaining market. This competition manifested itself most particularly in the repeated devaluations of the dollar, which have been carried out in an attempt to maintain or increase the overseas market for US exports and protect them and the US home market against the incursions of Germany and Japan, whose currencies have been revalued and have risen very markedly against the dollar. So far, however, the balance has not turned in favor of the United States on the world market. The decline of the dollar has, nevertheless cheapened US wage and property costs relative to those in Europe and Japan and has therefore reversed the flow of foreign investment, which is now going from these areas to the United States. Slack demand and increased competition has accelerated bankruptcies and monopolization nationally and aggressive export drives and renewed protectionism internationally.

Another major manifestation of overproduction and inadequate demand has been an increase in unutilized productive capacity in industry. This problem is particularly visible in the steel industry, which has been in a worldwide slump for some years and, after shutting down a number of steel mills, is still only working at 60 or 70 percent capacity in various parts of the industrialized world. In consequence, there has also been a marked slump in investments. With excess but unused capacity and low profits, business sees no good reason to engage in mammoth new investment. The 1973 level of investment in the industrialized economies was not regained until 1978, and still not in Britain today. Thus, there was a gaping investment hole from 1973 to 1978, and now investment is declining once again, because of a new recession. Moreover, the nature of investment has changed. Expansive investment to provide new productive capacity for more and new goods has increasingly been replaced by rationalizing investment designed to produce goods at reduced cost, particularly labor costs. There has been a lot of talk about new technology in the energy supply and in a number of other fields. Despite the fact that the price of energy shot up rapidly after 1973, and did so again in recent months, there have been no major new investments in the energy field. Prospecting and drilling for petroleum has increased markedly since 1973, but there has been no major new investment in petroleum refining, and this is a major reason for the recent bottlenecks. Also, there has been no major new investment in alternative sources of energy from shale oil, coal, or nuclear fuel. Economically, the nuclear industry is virtually in shambles; this explains much of the drive to sell nuclear reactors at home and abroad and has led to the strong competitive reactions and squabbles internationally (for example, between the United States and West Germany over Brazil and between the United States and France over Pakistan) and the stong antinuclear reaction in many parts of the world. All these alternative sources of energy, including solar energy and synthetic fuels, have been the subject of much talk, but so far it is all talk and no action. The main reason is that the general rate of profit and prospective markets do not yet justify any major investment in energy or in any other field. The apparent exception is the computer industry, particularly the use of microchips; so far it is primarily a rationalizing investment designed to reduce labor costs of production, and not a major new innovation that puts production on an entirely new footing. Before such an investment program with major new technology can be undertaken, the profit rate has to be elevated again, and that would entail vast economic, social, and political transformations on a world scale.

Instrumental in both the decline and possible future recovery of profits are another set of consequences and manifestations of this crisis. Since the mid-1960s, recessions have become more frequent, longer, deeper and more coordinated from one major industrial country to another. An index of the growth of these recessions is their impact on unemployment in the member countries of the Organization for Economic Cooperation and Development (OECD). In North America, Europe, Japan, Australia, and New Zealand registered unemployment rose to 5 million during the recession of 1967, in which the United States barely participated because it kept the wolf of recession from the door through the war against Vietnam. By the time of the recession of 1969–1971, which also hit the United States, registered unemployment had risen to 10 million in the industrialized countries. Unemployment then fell back to 8 million in the subsequent recovery from 1972 to 1973. In the next recession, which hit almost the whole capitalist world simultaneously from 1973 to 1975, and which was the deepest one so far since the 1930s, registered unemployment rose to 15 million in the industrialized countries, including 9 million (or roughly 9 percent of the labor force) in the United States. Since then, unemployment again declined to less than 6 million in the United States but continued to rise in the capitalist countries of Europe and Japan, as well as Canada and Australia. Indeed, the number of unemployed in these countries rose so much during the so-called recovery from 1975 to the present day that total OECD registered unemployment increased from 15 million at the bottom of the last recession to 17 or 18 million in 1979.

A new recession began in 1979–1980 in the United States and Britain and is visibly threatening elsewhere. No one knows for sure how long the recession will last. The Carter administration was talking about a so-called soft landing and hoped that the recession would be relatively mild and not very long, if only because 1980 is an election year. To the express dismay of President Carter, a confidential document leaked out of his administration, that objectively projects a much deeper recession lasting into 1981, with unemployment rising to at least 8 percent again.

There are very substantial reasons to anticipate that the current recession may be even more severe than the one in 1973–1975. This recession is much more welcome and "needed" than the previous one, which did not drive enough capital into bankruptcy to clean up the capitalist house sufficiently and did not successfully break the back of labor organization and militancy. Therefore, the capitalist states will do even less to combat this recession domestically than they did in the last one. The "debt economy," as *Business Week* aptly calls it, has grown so spectacularly that another further acceleration in the growth of debt threatens to increase the likelihood of a possible crash of the already excessively unstable financial house of cards; this has made worried bankers even more prudent and has reinforced economic conservatism. At the same time, the previously available financial and institutional bulwarks against the spread of recession, such as the development of speculative European and Asian currency markets, the counteractive flexible exchange rates, international coordination through economic summit conferences, and so forth, have already been substantially exhausted or have failed outright. Internationally, moreover, the safety valve that the socialist and OPEC countries offered capital through increased demand for Western exports is already significantly exhausted and much less likely to be available during this new recession. After their last expansion, and because of their limited capacity to pay, these economies have already had to restrict imports and are not likely to come to the rescue of Western capital again as they did after 1973. Thus, there would seem to be significant limits to consumer, investment, and export demand during this new recession. Thus increased military spending (and possibly other state-financed capital expenditures to develop new sources of energy) are the only other sources of additional demand; and the Iran and Afghanistan crises should be regarded more as justification than as causes for such expenditures.

Be that as it may, the new recession begins at a level of unemployment, particularly in Europe and Japan, that is vastly higher than the level prior to the 1973–1975 recession, and a level of investment that has only just regained the 1973 level. Serious "scientific" projections from official and institutional forecasters seem to be unable or unwilling to take due account of these factors in the preparation of their generally over-optimistic forecasts. The unexpected turn of events in 1979 and 1980 has obliged one international institution after another to undertake agonizing reappraisals and make downward revisions of their economic projections. For instance, the OECD was obliged to add an unnumbered page to its *Economic Outlook* after it went to press in order to lower its growth rate projections by 1 percent. The annual report of the International Monetary Fund prepared for its 1979 meeting predicted a long and hard worldwide recession starting in early 1980 as a consequence of the weakness of the US economy. During its annual meeting in Belgrade in September 1979, the IMF amended its 1980 forecast downward and said that "world economic growth will be lower than the precentage shown in the annual report." Since then, after the largest ever monthly decline—more than 4 percent—in the US index of economic indicators in April 1980, President Carter admitted that the new recession is more sudden, deeper, and apparently longer lasting than he and his advisors had foreseen. Economic research institutes in Germany and Britain finally issued reports expressing fears of slump conditions at home and abroad lasting at least into the mid-1980s. Moreover, this new recession comes on top of a weak recovery in which the economic, social, and political consequences of the last recession—including a legacy of over 17 million unemployed in the industrial capitalist countries— have not yet been overcome. This sobering circumstance is itself a mark of the deepening crisis.

Another manifestation—indeed an essential part—of this process of deepening crisis through successive recessions has been the attempt to reduce the cost of production through austerity policies, which have resulted in increased unemployment. Moreover, it can be demonstrated that in most industrial capitalist countries there has been a deliberate unemployment policy. Recessions are an essential part of the crisis of accumulation, which is an integral aspect of uneven capitalist development. But these recessions are demonstrably further promoted by policies made not only in Washington but also in London, Bonn, Paris, Tokyo, and elsewhere. For instance, when Paul Volcker, the new head of the Federal Reserve Board, was interviewed by the Senate, he said that he did not know if there was a recession yet, but come what may, the principal task is not combating recession, but combating inflation. What he meant in plain English is that he proposed to pursue, and would ask government to pursue, fiscal policies designed to restrain wages and decrease purchasing power in order to combat unemployment. Therefore, it is neither incidental nor accidental that Volcker's appointment was greeted with great jubilation in Bonn, Paris, and Tokyo, and in all other major financial and political capitals of the Western world.

Indeed, world capitalist political leaders, such as President Carter (who was elected on a "fight unemployment" platform but predictably soon switched to making "inflation the Public Enemy Number One" instead), Prime Minister Raymond Barre, British Labour ministers Callaghan and Healey, followed by their conservative successors Thatcher, Howe, and Joseph, and many others like them elsewhere have repeatedly declared that they would prefer to pursue conservative, deflationary fiscal policies to combat inflation even at the cost of rising unemployment and growing industrial shutdowns (as in the French steel mills, whose workers reacted vociferously).

The same argument is advanced everywhere: we need to hold down inflation because it hurts all of us at home equally (although inflation characteristically reduces real income from work and raises the real value of property) and particularly because inflation at home would price us out of the world market, cut our export capacity, and therefore create unemployment. The principal cause of inflation is, supposedly, high public spending and high wage demands (although wage costs are a small and declining component of selling prices, and the evidence shows that prices are pushed up by the attempt to protect profits in monopolized industry). These same arguments are used everywhere to defend the imposition of austerity policies, and to demand political restraint in public spending—except for defense and other business expenditures, of course—and in "responsibile" union wage demands, which are to be kept below the rate of inflation, with a resultant decline in real wages and income, especially at the lowest end of the income scale. In addition, however, to resting on very doubtful scientific grounds domestically, these arguments suffer from the logical fallacy of composition: when everybody pursues the same policy, as when everybody stands on tiptoe to see a passing parade, or when everyone cuts back on inflation, then nobody finds their relative position improved by their efforts—and everybody ends up worse off than before. The analogy, however, only goes so far: diminished comfort may be an entirely unintended consequence of crowd behavior, but lower wages definitely are not unintended consequences of herding people against inflation. Indeed, there is reason to believe that the principal economic purpose of the political slogan to fight inflation (which hurts everybody) at the cost of unemployment (which only hits some people directly) is not only to lower wages but also to weaken labor's power everywhere to defend its wage level and working conditions. In view of these official pronouncements and policies, it should come as no surprise that the world capitalist press has blithely summarized them in plain English by saying "The world needs a recession."

Austerity policies have been imposed in all the capitalist economies in an attempt to get workers to tighten their belts. This attempt has been more successful in some places than in others. Certainly in the United States and Britain real wages have gone down, while in other industrial economies there is conflicting evidence on wage rates. However, considering the increase in the number of unemployed, who receive no wages at all, then real wage receipts have fallen since 1973. At the same time, the capitalist world has made a concerted effort to cut welfare. The motto in the capitalist world today is to shift from "unproductive" to "productive" expenditures, including armaments of course; as for welfare: farewell. Another major attempt to cut production costs is to reorganize the work processes on the shop floor and in the office: in general, the new work processes involve speedup and downgrading the workers' skills.

These policies have been implemented wherever possible, and certainly in most parts of the Western world, through social democratic governments, often with the support of labor-oriented and Communist parties. Communist support of all kinds of capitalist austerity measures has been very visible in Italy and Spain. It is perhaps worth pointing out that in Spain it was even the secretary general of the Communist Party, Santiago Carillo, who took the initiative in proposing the Spanish austerity policy in the Pact of Moncloa after the election of Prime Minister Aldolfo Suarez. Austerity and incomes policies are also implemented in many places through the direct collaboration of labor and even Communist unions, as in Italy. The argument is to pursue a sort of lesser-evil policy, according to which it is better to tighten belts voluntarily than to be forced to do so by some right-wing or, as the Communists in Italy would say, fascist government. In some, indeed many, places these policies have led to considerable militancy on the shop floor and revolt of the mass base. This revolt has been particularly visible in Italy and Britain, where workers have rejected austerity policies which the union leadership had implemented. (The Spanish Communist Party and its unions have suddenly decided to oppose the austerity policy there as well, but to what extent?) In Britain, this very considerable militancy on and off the shop floor has made the newly elected Conservative government determined to put a tight rein on labor mobilization and the power of the unions through all kinds of legal action against picketing and other union organization, as well as through explicit policies to increase and use unemployment to discipline labor. In the past—and the right wing hopes that it will also be true in the future—a significant increase in unemployment makes militant union action increasingly difficult. Indeed, if capitalism is to recover "adequate" levels of profit and launch a renewed investment drive to bring it out of its present crisis of accumulation and into a new period of expansion, not only will it have to invest in a new technological base, but both the profitable introduction of new technology and such investment will have to be based on a major political defeat of labor, such as the defeat between the 1920s and 1940s.

These circumstances have led to very marked shifts to the right in most industrialized countries. The liberal candidacy of Edward Kennedy in the Democratic Party's presidential primaries was roundly defeated in the United States while President Carter swung sharply to the right on both domestic and foreign issues. Even the independent candidate John Anderson is very much of a conservative on fiscal and other domestic questions, while the Republican candidate, Ronald Reagan, is an archconservative. The even more right-wing Franz Joseph

Strauss is the conservative candidate for chancellor in West Germany. In Japan there has been a marked shift to the right and accelerating preparations for rearmament at the national level while Socialists and Communists have been all but eliminated from municipal and regional governments. The marked shifts to the right are not only manifest on this political level but in a whole variety of other fields such as in education, health, immigration, and civil rights legislation; in general, the "new right" is advancing by leaps and bounds on the ideological level in most industrial capitalist countries.

The American dream of bigger and better and continuous prosperity is finished in the United States and elsewhere in the West. In his July 15, 1979, speech on the crisis of confidence, President Carter said that the vast majority of Americans think the next five years will be worse than the last five. Carter's appraisal is quite realistic, but he might have added that the last five years have already been worse than the previous twenty-five. This crisis of confidence confronts the entire political spectrum with a growing ideological crisis of what to offer. The Carter speech is itself a manifestation of complete ideological bankruptcy. The only universal agreement in the commentary on Carter's speech was that he offered absolutely no solution to the crisis of confidence (which reflects the decline of American economic and political—in a word, imperialist—power) or even to the energy crisis which he said is a byproduct of this crisis.

The current situation has also brought on a crisis in economics, which, according to *Business Week,* is completely bankrupt as a source of forecasting, analysis, or policy. On the one hand, this bankruptcy manifests itself most visibly in stagflation—simultaneous unemployment and inflation—or in 1975 in "slumpflation"—in every Western capitalist country. On the other hand, the growth, inflation, and exchange rates fluctuate from one country to the next and repeatedly checkmate all attempts to analyze, let alone to regulate, the international monetary and economic system. The periodic "economic summits" held in France, Puerto Rico, London, Bonn, and now Tokyo among the leaders of the principal Western industrial

powers are no more than an open admission of this failure
of international economic coordination—and even analysis—
which is reminiscent of the complete failure of the World
Economic Conference held in London in 1931 during the last
great depression.

Keynesian economic theory only offers deflationary remedies for inflation or reflationary ones for unemployment. The
essential reason for the failure of Keynesianism is that it is
based on the assumption of competition while the increasingly
monopolized structure of the economy generates simultaneous
inflation and unemployment. Moreover, Keynesian policies
are essentially applicable to national economies in which governments can wield substantial regulatory influence. But the
world capitalist crisis is international and, since the relative
decline of US power, no single nation-state can stabilize the
world economy. Supranational institutions are equally useless
in the face of the speculative, private banking, Eurocurrency
market and nationalist state economic policies. It is ironic that
Keynesianism originated as a weapon to combat depression,
but became universally accepted and "successful" only during
(and because of!) the postwar expansion. At the first sign of
renewed world recession, Keynesian theory has proved itself
to be a snare and a delusion that has gone into immediate
bankruptcy. The resulting "post-Keynesian synthesis" is also
the theoretical reason for the reactionary exhumation of the
simplistic, neoclassical, and monetarist economic theory of the
1920s. This revival of old theory is highlighted by the award of
Nobel prizes in economics to Friedrich von Hayek, whose
theoretical work was done before the Great Depression, and
Milton Friedman, whose lone voice echoed in the wilderness
until the new world economic crisis put his unpopular and
antipopulist theories on the agenda of business board rooms
and government cabinet rooms in one capitalist country after
another. The real reason for the recent interest in fifty-year-
old theories is that capital now wants them to legitimize its
attack on the welfare state and "unproductive" expenditures
on social services, which capital claims to need for "productive" investment in industry, including armaments.

The onset of economic crisis, with low and sometimes negative growth rates, permanent inflation, and structural unemployment, and the reinstatement of outworn economic policies dating from the 1920s (and indeed 1890s) as emergency measures in the face of the bankruptcy of Keynesianism, as well as the drive to bid welfare farewell have generated a serious ideological crisis in the West. Right-wing and centrist political parties can no longer plausibly offer the bigger and better American way of life; and left-wing parties are afraid to offer a fundamental challenge to the former, lest the political center of gravity shift even further to the right or toward fascism in response. Thus, throughout the political spectrum in the West everybody's best offer is the lesser evil. In other words, a game of musical chairs develops in which every political party and faction rushes to sit in the just-vacated chair to the right, except that a few of them violate the rules of the game by moving two or three seats to the right at one jump, sowing confusion and making those who shift right more slowly appear to be almost radically left by comparison. But offering and choosing the lesser evil can only be a stopgap measure in the face of deepening crisis, until the political forces find a new, positive-sounding ideology with which to legitimize their retrograde and increasingly reactionary crisis policies. So far, such a new (national socialist?) ideology has not yet been developed, or at least has not found widespread reception. But what will happen after the next, perhaps deeper, recession, say by 1984? Will George Orwell's Big Brother be watching?

Development and modernization theory have proven inappropriate in the Third World, the gap between rich and poor is growing by leaps and bounds and even the number of poor and the depth of their poverty is increasing. The failures of these theories and models have now been publicly recognized by their strongest advocates, like Leontief for the United Nations, World Bank President Robert S. McNamara, and former US Secretary of State Henry Kissinger. In his 1977 address to the board of governors of the World Bank, President McNamara soberly observed:

Development, despite all the efforts of the past twenty-five
years, has failed to close the gap in per capita incomes between
developed and developing countries. . . . The proposition is
true. But the conclusion to be drawn from it is not that development efforts have failed, but rather that "closing the gap"
was never a realistic objective in the first place. . . . It was
simply not a feasible goal. Nor is it one today. . . . Even if
developing countries manage to double their per capita growth
rate, while the industrial world maintains its historical growth,
it will take nearly a century to close the absolute income gap
between them. Among the fastest growing developing countries, only seven would be able to close the gap within a
hundred years, and only another nine within a thousand years.

However, since the 1973–1975 recession, the growth rate in
the developed capitalist countries has declined; and the growth
rate of the non-petroleum exporting countries in the Third
World has been cut in half.

For the world's poor the past has been dismal and future
prospects are dim. The 1978 *World Development Report* of the
World Bank observes on its first page:

The past quarter century has seen great progress in developing
countries. . . . But much remains to be accomplished. Most
countries have not yet completed the transition to modern
economies and societies, and their growth is hindered by a
variety of domestic and international factors. Moreover, about
800 million people still live in absolute poverty. These people
are living at the very margin of existence—with inadequate
shelter, education, and health care. . . . Many of these people
have experienced no improvement in their living standards;
and in countries where economic growth has been slow, the
living standards of the poor may even have deteriorated.

But as recent events in Iran and the end of the "miracle" in
Brazil suggest, even with rapid growth here and there, one
economic miracle and take-off into development after another
turns out to be a snare and a delusion really based on ruthless
exploitation, cruel oppression, and the marginalization from
"development" for the majority of the population. This experience, which is only sharpened by the present crisis, has

now raised the most serious doubts about the very concept of development as a progressive, integral, and integrating social process in that part of the world which used to be called backward, poor, or colonial and then—through successive euphemisms—undeveloped, underdeveloped, developing, new, emerging, and less developed. At the same time, though structural impediments to development and dependence certainly remain real in the Third World, the usefulness of structuralist, dependence, and new dependence theories of underdevelopment as guides to policy seems to have been undermined by the world crisis of the 1970s. The Achilles' heel of these conceptions of dependence has always been the implicit, and sometimes explicit, notion of some sort of "independent" alternative for the Third World. This theoretical alternative never existed, in fact—certainly not on the noncapitalist path and now apparently not even through so-called socialist revolutions. The new crisis of real world development now renders such partial development and parochial dependence theories and policy solutions invalid and inapplicable.

The recent call for national or collective self-reliance (but without autarchy) within a capitalist "new international economic order" appears to be the consequence of ideological desperation. For instance, Angola still relies heavily on the payments of foreign exchange that the US Gulf Oil Company makes for petroleum produced in Cabinda under the protection of troops from Cuba. In the meantime, with regard to Tanzania, the model of self-reliance in Africa, *Business Week* (December 25, 1978) states that its economy is on the brink of collapse, while the *International Herald Tribune* (May 7, 1979) reports: "Amid economic difficulties, Tanzania [is] seen improving ties to US [and] is taking a new look at Western finance and expertise." No wonder that Tanzanian president Nyerere commemorated the tenth anniversary of his proclamation of the goal of self-reliance and *ujamaa* in the Arusha Declaration by soberly observing that "Tanzania is certainly neither socialist nor self-reliant. . . . Our nation is still economically dependent. . . . [The goal of socialism] is not even in sight" (*International Herald Tribune*, April 21, 1977).

The Third World was and is an integral and important part of the world capitalist economy. Unless the working class in the West and in the South can prevent it, the Third World is destined to carry the major part of the burden in international capital's attempt to reverse the tide of the growing economic crisis. In the first place, since the Third World is an integral part of the capitalist world, the crisis has been immediately transmitted from the center to the Third World through growing balance of payments deficits. As demand in the industrialized countries declined or grew more slowly, so did prices for exported raw materials other than petroleum. At the same time, the vast world inflation in the industrialized economies increased prices of manufactured commodities imported by the Third World. Therefore, despite a temporary raw-materials price boom in 1973 (which was completely reversed after 1974), the terms of trade have been shifting once again and the non-petroleum exporting Third World countries have faced increasingly serious balance of payments problems and a mushrooming foreign debt. Moreover, it is no accident that from 1974 to 1978 the OPEC surplus was more or less equivalent to the increase in the balance of payments deficit of the Third World, suggesting that most of the increase in the prices of petroleum since 1973 has ultimately been born by the Third World.

A significant portion of the OPEC surplus has been recycled through the banks in the metropolitan imperialist countries to the Third World to cover their balance of payments deficits through private loans at increasingly onerous costs. Their growing debt is then used as a political instrument to impose harsh austerity policies in the Third World. This blackmail through debt renegotiation and extension has received considerable newspaper coverage in the cases of Turkey, Peru, Zaire, and Jamaica, but it has also become standard International Monetary Fund (IMF) and private bank operating procedure throughout the Third World. Thus, the IMF will set certain conditions: if the government does not devalue its currency to make exports and foreign investment cheaper, lower wages, cut the government budget especially for welfare expenditures, and take other unpopular measures, and if it does not replace Minister A with Minister B, who is more likely to institute the IMF-supported policies, then the country will not get the IMF certificate of good behavior, and without it neither official loans nor loans from private banks will be forthcoming. This political-economic club has been used to beat governments into shape and force them to adopt policies of super-austerity throughout the Third World. However, the same thing has also happened in Portugal and Great Britain: when the IMF, led by the United States, offered Britain a $3.9 billion loan in 1976, it gave Britain virtually the same treatment as had previously been reserved for banana republics— perhaps that is an indication that Britain is becoming a sort of pseudo-Third World country. Again, however, just as unemployment and recession are not simply, or even primarily, due to government policy decisions, neither are austerity measures in the Third World simply the result of pressure from the industrialized capitalist countries. These external political pressures are simply reinforcing tendencies that have another, much broader, economic base, namely, the capitalist attempt to maintain or revive the rate of profit by producing at lower costs in the Third World (and in the socialist countries), with national political support for these repressive measures.

Costs of production are reduced mainly by moving labor-intensive industries, but also some very capital-intensive industries, such as steel and automobiles, to the Third World. It is perhaps symbolic that the Volkswagen Beetle is now made in Mexico, not Germany, for export to other parts of the world. From the point of view of the world capitalist economy, this is a transfer of a portion of industrial production from high-cost to low-cost areas. From the point of view of the Third World, this move represents a policy of export promotion, particularly of nontraditional industrial exports. Third World export promotion has two seemingly different origins. On the one hand, the economies that had advanced most in the process of import substitution, like India, Brazil, and Mexico, have turned these import substitutes into export manufactures, from textiles to automobiles, some produced by multinational firms. On the other hand, foreign capital went to other Third World countries to set up manufacturing facilities to produce solely for export, rather than for the domestic market. This movement started in the 1960s with Mexico (which combined both kinds of industry but in different regions), South Korea, Taiwan, Hong Kong, and Singapore. In the 1970s it spread to Malaysia, the Philippines, and increasingly from India, Pakistan, Sri Lanka, Egypt, Tunisia, Morocco, the Ivory Coast to virtually every country in the Caribbean. These economies offer cheap labor, and they compete among one another with state subsidies to provide plant facilities, electricity, transportation, tax relief, and every other kind of incentive for foreign capital to produce there for the world market. In the case of Chile, the military junta went so far as to offer to pay part of the otherwise starvation wages, so that foreign capital could keep its costs down.

In order to provide these low wages, and indeed to reduce the wages from one country to another in the competitive bid to offer more favorable conditions to international capital, these governments need to destroy the labor unions, and to prohibit strikes and other union activity. Systematic imprisonment, torture, and assassination of labor and political leaders, the imposition of emergency rule, martial law, and military government is used in one Third World country after another. Indeed, the whole state apparatus has to be adapted to this Third World role in the new international division of labor.

This repressive movement has swept systematically through Asia, Africa, and Latin America in the course of the 1970s and demonstrably is not simply due to some kind of autonomous political force to combat Communism (which has become a rather doubtful policy anyway, at a time when even the United States has socialist allies and some socialist countries collaborate with these repressive regimes). This repressive political policy has very clear economic purposes and functions—to make these economies more competitive on the world market by lowering wages and to surpress those elements of the local bourgeoisie who are tied to the internal market. This sector of the bourgeoisie pressured for certain kinds of mild restrictions of the operations of multinational corporations in a number of Third World countries during the late 1960s and early 1970s. Since then, these restrictions have increasingly been removed, and one government after another is falling over itself to offer favorable conditions to international capital.

The motto now is to work for the world market rather than for the internal market. Effective demand on the national market is not, and is not intended to be, the source of demand for national production; demand on the world market is, and is intended to be, the source of market demand. Therefore there is no reason to raise the wages of the direct producers, because they are not destined to purchase the goods that they produce. Instead the goods are supposed to be purchased on the world market far away. An important exception is the small local market of the high-income receivers, which is supposed to expand. Thus, there is a polarization of income, not only between developed and underdeveloped countries on the global level but also on the national level, with the poor getting poorer and the rich getting richer. In some cases, as in Brazil until 1974, the attempt to develop a high-income market for part of local industry has been very successful. However, in Brazil as elsewhere in the Third World, this "development model" is based on the depression of the wage rate—wages have been cut by about half in Brazil, Uruguay, Argentina, and Chile and are being forced down in Peru and elsewhere—and the forced marginalization and unemployment of labor. Both of these processes are rapidly increasing the immiseration of the masses and the polarization of society in the Third World. Moreover, since in general the internal market is being restrained and restricted, the sector of the bourgeoisie that depends on the internal market, as in Chile and Argentina, also has to be repressed. Therefore, big capital must institute a military government that will repress not only labor but also a sector of the bourgeoisie and of the petty bourgeoisie. The governing alliance is between the sector of local capital allied with international capital and their military and political executors. This arrangement involves a very substantial reorganization of the state in the Third World, and often its militarization, so that the Third World can more effectively participate in the international division of labor.

Now in some places since late 1976, in others since 1977 and 1978, there appears to have been a reversal of this tendency toward military coups, emergency rule, and martial law. There have been elections in India and Sri Lanka, pseudo-elections in Bangladesh and the Philippines, elections in Ghana and Nigeria, elections or their announcements in various parts of Latin America, and some perhaps significant liberalization in the military regime in Brazil. Some people attribute these developments to President Carter's human rights policy, though it is a bit difficult to sustain the efficacy of his human rights policy when in quite a few crucial cases it either was absent or was restrained in the "higher national interest." Other people attribute the liberalization to increasing mass mobilization in many parts of the Third World. Still others attribute these apparent changes to a supposed failure of the new policy of export promotion and—certainly according to many Brazilians—to the renewed importance of a policy of import substitution and the widening of the internal market. However, at this time any such redirection of the Third World economies is hardly noticeable. Renewed import substitution in the Third World would be objectively aided and abetted by a far-reaching protectionist drive and the substantial breakdown of the system of international trade and finance elsewhere in the world. As the world economic crisis deepens, this eventuality is admittedly a distinct possibility, but so far it has not come to pass. In the Third World, progressive import substitution of consumer goods—though less so of capital goods produced for the export market—would require a relatively more equal distribution of income and a politically more benign regime to permit a broader coalition of classes. In other words, these people argue that the dark days of the mid-1970s are over, and that we are again facing the prospect of a redemocratization, or at least limited democracy, in many parts of the Third World. Even this measure of democracy would offer better conditions for popular mobilization and for the continuation or acceleration of national liberation movements and of socialist revolutions in one country after another in the Third World.

On the other hand, it may also be argued with considerable evidence that these recent developments do *not* represent the reversal of the emerging new model of economic integration of the Third World in the international division of labor in response to the development of the world crisis, but that this apparent redemocratization is simply the institutionalization of this new model of economic growth based on export promotion. Severe political repression is the midwife to this new model; but once the model is in place, it is possible to ease off a bit on political repression. Then, indeed, it is not only possible but politically necessary and desirable to get a wider social base for the political regime and to institute a kind of limited political democracy by handing over the government from military to civilian rule. But these political modifications would not be made in order to overturn the present economic order and again promote import substitution, let alone so-called noncapitalist growth or some variety of "socialism." Instead, their purpose would be to maintain and institutionalize the insertion of the Third World into the international division of labor as low-wage producers during the present world economic crisis. If we look realistically at what is happening in Asia, Africa, and Latin America, there is very considerable economic and political evidence for this latter explanation.

A political counterpart of this economic alternative is a renewed populist alliance of labor and bourgeois popular forces and parties. This alliance would press for the amelioration of politically repressive regimes and their gradual replacement by superficially more democratic, but essentially technocratic, ones to implement the same fundamentally exclusivist and antipopulist economic policy. In the pursuit of such unholy alliances around the Third World, it now seems opportune to resurrect all kinds of bygone politicians. These politicians did not have left-wing support in their heyday, and did not pursue very progressive policies, but they now receive support from the left to implement policies that are far more rightist than their previous ones. These rightist policies now appear as the lesser evil compared to the policies of the current (often military) governments. Therefore, for lack of better alternatives the opposition is now rallying behind political figures like

Eduardo Frei in Chile, Siles Suarez in Bolivia, Fernando Belaúnde Terry in Peru, Awolowo and Azikwe in Nigeria, Benigno Aquino in the Philippines, Pramoj in Thailand, Indira Gandhi in India, and even the ghost of Ali Bhutto in Pakistan to lead "progressive" movements that are likely to maintain the essentials of the status quo and certainly will not offer any real development alternatives.

To the extent that these policies and politicians are a realistic political alternative around the Third World, orthodox development theory and ideology, as well as progressive dependence or even new dependence theory—not to mention the Chinese "Three Worlds" theory and the Soviet "noncapitalist" way to national liberation, democracy, and varieties of socialism—are all completely bankrupt. Under these circumstances, today none of these theories and ideologies can offer any realistic policy alternatives and practical political economic guidelines for the pursuit of economic development or national liberation, let alone of socialist construction. Independent national development in the Third World has proved to be a snare and a delusion; and self-reliance, collective or otherwise, is a myth that is supposed to hide this sad fact of life in the world capitalist system. These political compromises of the avowedly revolutionary socialist, and particularly the Communist Party, left around the Third World are another measure of the ideological crisis of the left in the face of the present world crisis.

Stalinist theories of historical progression by inevitable stages through feudalism, capitalism, socialism, and Communism; the transitional existence of two world markets, one capitalist and the other socialist; and the post-Stalin Soviet amendment proposing a "noncapitalist path" in the transition to socialism have certainly been relegated to the dustbin of history by experience. Khrushchev's hope of "burying" the West has itself been buried; and the Soviet Union is trying to compensate for its comparative economic, political, and ideological weakness (even more evident in the "popular democracies" of Eastern Europe) through increasing military strength, thus threatening not only its potential enemies in the West but also its supposed allies in the East. The Maoist theory and practice of "new democracy," "walking on two legs," Cultural Revolution, and Three Worlds (two superpowers, the other industrialized countries, and the Third World including China) have been seriously challenged by events inside and outside China and have recently been denounced even by the erstwhile faithful Albanian Workers Party. The international (albeit not universal) sympathy with the models of Cuban guerrilla and popular movements, Korean *juche* self-reliance, and Vietnamese national liberation have given way to searching critiques and heartfelt doubts among many of their previously enthusiastic supporters around the world. Trotskyist and new left movements of many varieties have left a trail of disillusioned or disaffected militants to be reintegrated into the establishment. Now, after the largely self-inflicted electoral defeats of the Communist parties in France, Spain, Italy, and even Japan on the municipal level, observers from left to right are writing Eurocommunism off as neither European nor Communist while it lasted. The secretary general of the French Communist Party, Georges Marchais, issued "denials" of Eurocommunism's demise at the May 1979 party congress, which also celebrated the end of the left alliance with the socialists and followed Marchais's lead in another about-turn toward Moscow.

In the meantime, Deng Xiaoping's theatrics on his 1979 tour of the United States to get Western technology and credit for the drive to make China a world industrial power by the year 2000 only highlight Chinese developments over the last decade. Since the defeat of the Cultural Revolution and the downfall of Lin Biao in 1971 (apparently for favoring a rapprochement with the Soviet Union instead of with the United States), the way was cleared for Zhou Enlai's "conciliatory" line of ping-pong diplomacy, the invitation to Nixon to visit China, the launching of the Four Modernizations (agriculture, industry, science and technology, and defense), no longer through self-reliance as with foreign aid and trade (which more than quadrupled in the 1970s and 85 percent of which is with capitalist countries), the rehabilitation of Liu Shaoqi, and reinstatement of the capitalist-roader victims of the Cultural Revolution, led by Deng Xiaoping. Now he is taking China on a "great leap backward" to 1957, the year before the Great Leap Forward, in order to get a better running start for the leap to great-power status in the twenty-first century.

In the wake of their own economic and related political problems, the "socialist" economies of the Soviet Union and Eastern Europe are implementing a detente with the West (albeit in competition with China) to import Western technology and pay for it with exports produced by cheap labor through thousands of bipartite and tripartite production agreements with Western firms and Third World countries. Even so, the East European and Soviet demand for Western technology is growing so rapidly that their cumulative debt to the West has grown from $8 billion in 1972 to over $60 billion in 1979, despite the Eastern balance of payments surplus with the South, which the East uses in part to offset its deficit with the West. Moreover, as Brezhnev has correctly observed, "because of the broad economic links between capitalist and socialist countries, the ill effects of the current crisis in the West have also had an impact on the socialist world." And therefore, his colleague and chairman of the Bulgarian State Council, Todor Zhivkov, adds, "it may be hoped that the crisis in the West may come to a rapid end." The crisis continues, however; and the European socialist economies grew only half as fast as the last five-year plans called for, and in some of them output actually declined in 1979. Not only do the Eurocommunist parties hope the crisis will go away; for their part they also help capital to overcome the crisis economically by imposing austerity measures on labor, as in Spain and Italy, and overcome the crisis politically by strengthening the state and its repressive power, which the Communist Party of Italy is now the first to defend and expand.

One wonders how the official pronouncements of self-styled Communist and revolutionary socialist centers, parties, and movements can continue to claim that "the situation is excellent" (Beijing), "socialism is advancing stronger than ever" (Moscow), and "revolutionary possibilities are around the corner" at least in southern Europe (Trotskyists). This is particu-

larly surprising in the face of the domestic and foreign policies—repression at home and wars abroad—that mark contemporary socialist countries, Communist parties, and revolutionary movements caught in the grip of a grave crisis of
Marxism that is costing the cause of socialism countless millions of supporters around the world.

The current ideological and political dilemma of socialism
derives from, and may be summarized by, the complete abandonment of the famous means and end of the *Manifesto of the
Communist Party:* Workers of the world, unite! Both the theory
and the practice of proletarian internationalism as a means to
the goal of communism have been replaced by "socialism in
one country—mine." Moreover, communism has been replaced by socialism as the end goal of social development.
Though for Marx, Engels, and Lenin socialism meant no more
than an unstable transitional stage on the road to communism,
it has been converted into an end station or steady state. Some
socialists claim to have arrived already, and other, more realistic
ones (ironically called "idealists" by the former), such as Mao
Zedong, only claim that their country is in transition to socialism. In "prerevolutionary" Chile it was customary to talk of the
transition to the transition to socialism, before the military
coup violently destroyed these illusions and placed only "restricted democracy" on the agenda as the distant goal to be
achieved. In an attempt to escape a similar fate, the Eurocommunists proposed a "historic compromise" as their goal. Of
course, if socialism no longer means the transition to communism through proletarian internationalism but becomes an
established state in one country and a distant goal in others, the
definition of a socialist state and the means of achieving it
become endlessly debatable. Thus, socialists become like the
person who looks for his lost watch only under the nearest
streetlight, because he claims that he can see it there quicker
and better, although the watch for socialism was lost some-
where else down another road and has made the time of
communism recede back into infinite darkness.

The more the Marxist theory that is supposed to guide and
justify this socialist practice is examined under the plain light

of day, the more indistinguishable does Marxism become from the orthodox, everyday, bourgeois capitalist theory and practice of "national development." It is ironic in view of the stated goals of Marxism—but perhaps not surprising in terms of its analysis—that since the state-promoted capitalist ascension of noncolonial Japan into the charmed circle of industrial powers, outside the West only the "socialist" countries have been able to achieve, or as now in the case of China realistically aspire to, participation in the world capitalist economy on a basis that is even remotely equal to that of the developed capitalist countries. *None* of the Third World countries have escaped dependent capitalist underdevelopment, nor do any of them show any prospects of doing so in the foreseeable future, despite Brazilian, Korean, Iranian, or Mexican miracles or oil booms. Only some "socialist" economies can now knock on the door of or challenge the capitalist inner sanctum, because they were temporarily relatively isolated from the capitalist international division of labor. Their isolation was not—oh, double irony— by their own choice, but mainly because the capitalist powers forced it on them during the Cold War in reaction to their socialist transformations of domestic property, productive, and political relations, which is the other reason for their success. Even the most nationalist, dependent, and state capitalist Third World countries like Nasser's Egypt never attempted that. However, if China, Vietnam, Yugoslavia, Hungary, Poland, and perhaps last but not least the Soviet Union are any guide, the further irony is that, driven on by their own internal economic and political crises, these countries do not want to use "socialism" to challenge the West in its time of crisis; rather, they want to join the capitalist world system as nationalist competitive partners on as nearly equal terms as possible and in the process lend the capitalists an economic, political, and thereby also ideological hand in overcoming the world crisis of capitalism. Someone in East Germany suggested that socialists would win the race with the West as soon as they stopped running in the same direction. But as long as they play tag instead, the socialist countries, and with them the cause of socialism in much of the world, will remain caught in a dilemma of damned if they do and damned if they don't. Or is this Catch-22 simply the inevitable end of treading the path of "socialism in one country," while confronting the cruel ironies of an ancient triple Greek tragedy in the guise of the modern world system?

A number of questions present themselves about the further development and resolution of the world crisis or crises and about the theory to guide their interpretation and the ideology to influence their practice. Here and now it is only possible to pose some of these questions and to leave their answers open to further reflection in the near future, and perhaps to resolution or reformulation by hindsight in the more distant future.

Current developments pose the following questions in technical terms for historians, sociologists, economists, and Marxists, and in more general terms for political policymakers and the public: Are there numerous particular crises in many societies or aspects of life, or is there a general crisis—in the sense of the definition quoted in our opening paragraph—in a single world system? Are the crises recurrent occasional or cyclical ones, subject to possible resolution, or does the development of crisis represent a step—even the last step—toward a general crisis that spells the end of the capitalist world system? Implicit in our observations and formulations is the suggestion of a single world capitalist system, which is undergoing another in a series of long, cyclical crises, from which it will likely recover through far-reaching and fundamental economic, social, political, and cultural readjustments; but this crisis and its resolution also contributes to the cumulative degeneration and, after successive crises, the ultimate dissolution of world capitalism in the still unforseeable future.

Does the present crisis pose the economic alternative between increasing market demand to expand profitability and reducing costs of production through increasing exploitation to deepen profitability (in Marxist terms, realization of value versus raising surplus value)? Does the crisis pose this alternative in such a way as to oblige capital and labor to opt for the second alternative of greater exploitation with less employment and public demand, *before* the first alternative of renewed expansion can again become a realistic possibility as a result, precisely, of the prior rationalization and exploitation? Does this option of—or imperative for—world capitalist recovery imply or require a temporary increase in capitalist exploitation or extraction of surplus value through reduction of the work force, reorganization and speedup of the work process at lower real wages for the remaining workers, and reduced welfare for the population in general in favor of monopoly capital in the industrial capitalist countries? Does the same resolution of the capitalist crisis also involve the relocation of some industrial processes based on the increase in superexploitation in the Third World? Does the same resolution of the world crisis of capital accumulation imply or require the accelerated reintegration of the "socialist" economies and "feudal" OPEC countries and virgin lands into the world capitalist economy, both as sources of additional surplus value and as sources of demand, in part to compensate the demand restrictions in the developed and "developing" sectors of the world economy? And does this process imply the extension or intensification of the operation of world market forces (*and* of the law of value in Marxist terms) from the center of the world capitalist economy *into* the socialist economies and to populations and spaces (in the Middle East, Amazonia, Siberia, the polar regions, the seabed, and even outer space) that previously were effectively beyond the frontiers of the world capitalist system? Does this process represent an expansion of the "internal frontiers" of capital, analogous to the expansion of the "external frontiers" in response to each of the previous major world crises of capital accumulation? Does this progressive change from expanding to deepening capital imply further development or the beginning of the end of capitalism? What is the time scale of this process of development and degeneration?

It is too early to answer the last question, if only because the rise and fall of capitalism depends in part on the social resistance to its development and the generation of contrary or alternative political forces and developments. The political process has not yet run its course, even in the resolution of the present crisis, let alone in the subsequent development or degeneration of capitalism and its alternatives. However, this political process already raises a number of further questions about prospects and policy for the immediate future.

We have already suggested that the politically reactionary, conservative, and social democratic forces in the West and South (and perhaps in the East) face crises of economic theory, political ideology, and social policy for which they themselves have as yet found no solution. Pre-Keynesian neoclassical and monetarist economic theory, fascist political ideology, and nineteenth-century liberal social policy seem to offer renewed frames of reference and points of attraction (despite their mutual contradictions) in the absence of a viable alternative to the growing unreality of the American-cum-Keynesian way of life. However, new situations will eventually require new propositions, and who knows what combination of extant liberal, technocratic, and corporativist doctrines, as well as totally new ones, will win the day? The resistance to capitalist rationalization and reorganization from labor, socialist, environmental, feminist, ethnic and nationalist, religious and rejectionist forces is considerable, but highly divided and very confused. So far, they have not been able to formulate sufficiently attractive ideological alternatives. Viable resistance, let alone realistic alternatives, from the labor and socialist opposition to contemporary capitalist reorganization seems to be decreasing rather than increasing. Certainly throughout the world social democratic and Marxist theory and ideology and labor, socialist, and Communist party policy face severe crises of direction and of legitimacy. Alternative environmental and feminist forces are growing; but the more they grow, the more do their demands seem to become compatible with the exigencies of capital and the more is their leadership co-opted into the political establishment.

By far the strongest and most massive social mobilization in the world today has been taking place under ethnic, nationalist, and religious banners. Many of these movements are expressions of resistance to the present capitalist and socialist orders and to the attempts at their rationalization. Ethnic regionalist and nationalist movements have achieved greater mass mobilization and expression of discontent with the economic situation than any direct "economic" or "political" challenges to the status quo. Demands for autonomy or sovereignty, and nationalist, chauvinist, and jingoist appeals, have been finding increasing mass support. Yet many of these movements are manipulated by the capitalist right and divide the labor left, few of them challenge state power per se, and none of them reject participation in the international division of labor of the world capitalist economic system.

Religious conviction combined with nationalist sentiment, as in Poland, Iran, and Afghanistan have permitted the Catholic Pope John Paul II and the Muslim Ayatollah Ruhollah Khomeini to mobilize millions of people to a far greater extent than other ideologies and leaders, although parts of Asia, Africa, and the Caribbean have also been experiencing progressive mobilization under socialist banners. All of these movements, which are likely to intensify in the coming years, are expressions of growing popular frustration with the political and economic policies enacted in response to the crisis. To that extent, these movements represent antisystemic resistance to the reorganization of the world system by capital and for capital accumulation. In all of these movements the preponderant force in the mixture seems to be based less on socialist, that is, anticapitalist, politics or even on religious convictions of integrity or rejection of competing ideologies, and most strongly on nationalist sentiments of identity in opposition to foreign interest and influence. How centrifugal these opposition movements really are remains an open question. How the capitalist system will respond to efforts to destroy it—and whether there are any alternatives to the capitalist world system—remains to be seen.

9. LET'S NOT WAIT FOR 1984: DISCUSSION OF THE CRISIS

Andre Gunder Frank and Samir Amin

IL MANIFESTO: You have read what we have written on the new character of the crisis and the strategic orientation we are proposing. To organize the discussion, we should first of all state its purpose: first, an analysis of the crisis, and second, what a valid response might be.

We find it useful to raise several questions regarding the crisis. First, is the current crisis, however serious it may appear, one of those conjunctural or cyclical crises from which capitalism can emerge by means of restructuring which does not imply substantial modification of its political and social framework? Second, does this crisis, like the one in 1929, mean that there will be a long period of economic and social instability, fascism, and conflict among states? Third, can one predict that capitalism will enter a new upswing through changes in the international division of labor, in the social equilibrium, and in internal political rules, as it did after World War II (even though this may occur with a great deal of agitation and conflict)?

When we bring up this last hypothesis, we are obviously not thinking in terms of Italy but rather about the possibility of restructuring on a world scale. The impetus for such restructuring would come from the United States, and it would open up new frontiers for capitalist development in the Third World and around the Soviet Union. The fourth, more general, question refers to our ideas about the specificity of the current crisis, which we see developing as a moment in a historical

This is an English translation of an interview that was originally published in the Italian journal *Il Manifesto* in February 1974. It was translated by Mimi Keck.

phase, characterized by a more general crisis of the whole capitalist system. By that we mean this historical formation's current inability—even in moments of "prosperity"—to satisfy people's historically determined needs and to exercise hegemony over the masses, at least those in the industrial regions. The political importance of this hypothesis lies in the fact that one can derive from this specificity the relevance of a revolutionary perspective now, even at the center of the system. This would constitute an important difference from previous crises, where the system's weak links were in peripheral or relatively peripheral areas. This last question touches on the problem of the capitalist system's "historicity," and therefore on its degeneration and the exhaustion of its historical function over time. We would add, for the sake of clarity, that this seems to us to have very little to do with "breakdown" theories.

ANDRE GUNDER FRANK: There has been a great deal of discussion among Samir, myself, and other economists on all these problems, and we will try to summarize it. Personally, I have a lot of doubts about the exhaustion of capitalism's historical function and about the beginning of a phase of degeneration. I think that today the capitalist system has to seek new frontiers for its development in the Third World and in the countries which gravitate around the USSR. The problem consists in knowing whether this search can result in anything, and the extent to which such an outcome could help the system overcome the presently insurmountable problems within its center area. In other words, the extension of capitalism to areas in the periphery and in the so-called socialist world would be a "natural" strategy for the system. But for a more organic contribution, it would be better for Samir to sum up the sense of our recent discussions around the questions you are asking.

IL MANIFESTO: But what do you think is the most salient characteristic of the present crisis?

FRANK: I think that it is a classic accumulation crisis, though it might be an accumulation crisis grafted onto a decadent phase of the system, something which became very visible in 1914. The crisis appeared at an international level in 1967, when the rate of profit fell, and inevitably got worse, not in 1974 but in the following years. In effect, I envisage a long period of crisis, analogous to, but not the same as, the one that went from 1914 to 1945, with all the disorder that it brought. One can also find analogies to the 1873–1895 crisis, which witnessed the birth of imperialism.

IL MANIFESTO: To what can we attribute the falling rate of profit?

SAMIR AMIN: In a very schematic way, which presages agreement with some of your hypotheses, it could be attributed to the exhaustion of one model of accumulation and, therefore, the need for another model, which is difficult to delineate clearly within the capitalist system. But let me try to respond to your questions in a more orderly fashion.

First of all, I must emphasize the fact that for me this is a structural crisis in the real sense of the term. It is neither a conjunctural crisis, nor a normal recessive phase, nor a demand for simple readjustments to the energy price increase, nor even a pure demand crisis for restrictions of expenditures within the framework of the system. This is a crisis which affects the current accumulation model, its base of social support, the balance between the capitalist mode of production and the internal and external peripheral areas. A crisis, in sum, which puts modes of production, the political framework, and systems of social alliance on trial.

IL MANIFESTO: In other words, a crisis that capitalism cannot get out of by reducing wages or instituting repressive policies in some areas of the world, but which implies conflicts analogous to those that took place in the period beginning in the 1930s, which ended up effecting a change in the accumulation model?

AMIN: When the development of the productive forces enters into contradiction with the relations of production, this tends to impose an *overall* restructuring, not only in technical and economic areas but also in the social and political alliances which correspond to the existing accumulation model. The dates with which we might compare the current crisis historically are 1848, 1871, and 1917. But what we are interested in emphasizing is the fact that in such periods of crisis, tension, imbalance, and attempts to readjust, there is a rebirth of political life, and space opens up for revolutionary activity. Thus 1848 produced the *Manifesto of the Communist Party,* 1871 the Paris Commune, 1917 the October Revolution and later, the vast changes in China.

IL MANIFESTO: However, 1929 did not open up a revolutionary breach.

AMIN: It's not the year 1929 that we have to be concerned with, but the whole period from 1914 to 1945: World War I, a "worse than nothing" style economic recovery, the October Revolution, fascism, and World War II, which thrust the US model, with its twenty-five years of extraordinary development, onto the industrial world. The crises indicate the different periods in the history of the capitalist system, each one of which has a given system of social alliances. Without going back to the beginning, 1848 marks the extension of capitalism, which up to that point was limited to England, northern France, and Belgium. With 1848 and the *Manifesto,* the proletariat became conscious for the first time. This was quickly overcome by the fantastic expansion of capitalism in Europe: Italian unity, the Austro-Hungarian empire, railroads, corporations— in sum, a more advanced stage in the development of the productive forces.

FRANK: And all this on the basis of changes that took place during the crisis itself, the achievement of new technological levels, new internal relations among the bourgeoisies and among the different productive sectors.

AMIN: After 1870 we had imperialism, the monopolies, world expansion, then the long period from 1914 to 1945 and after that the US model. The basis for capitalist development over the last twenty-five years has been European and Japanese recovery with respect to the United States, a recovery which brought with it a whole series of things: the challenge to the United States, the myths of technocracy and of Europe, and so forth, and all this in a phase characterized by a deep crisis of Marxism and of the workers' movement. This is a type of development which has now entered into crisis.

FRANK: This was a type of development based on particularly dynamic and technologically specific industries like petrochemicals, electronics, and cybernetics, which now do not appear to offer long-term development potentials, that is, a satisfactory return on investment. For the same reason, I think that in order to renew its development, the system currently needs to discover new technological bases, as well as social and political ones.

AMIN: A new technological base presupposes changes in intersectoral relations and, therefore, in relations among the different capitalist powers. That is, it assumes a modification of the international division of labor and of corresponding domestic social alliances.

FRANK: The fact that it is socially and technologically impossible to go on in the old way is what presents capitalism with the opportunity to restructure itself, and the popular forces with the opportunity to prevent it from doing so.

IL MANIFESTO: How important do you consider two characteristics of the current accumulation model which we think are important: (1) the extreme concentration of directly productive sectors and productivity in general, and (2) the application of science to an increasingly restricted area of society? In cruder terms, the restriction of the productive area and the extension of the nonproductive one.

AMIN: I can answer that right away. Let's not forget that the period from 1914 to 1945 was one of the longest and most violent periods of crisis. The ensuing period presents very singular and limiting characteristics: the accumulation process was not yet dominated by a simple balance between Sector I (production of capital goods) and Sector II (production of consumer goods), but rather required the extraordinary development of a Sector III, nonproductive consumption, which ranged from military spending to the parasitic nature of the tertiary sector, to real estate speculation, and so on. In fact, the balance between supply and demand—or realization—required the extraordinary rapid growth of an area of parasitism, which has limited the meaning of development over the last twenty-five years. This is the first characteristic. The second characteristic is that over the last twenty-five years development has brought with it a progressive reduction of capitalism's social base, for which the dominant groups in Western Europe and Japan have tried to compensate by integrating the working class. But that is precisely where the greatest problems have shown up, such that Western Europe and Japan, after having failed at this operation, have gone into crisis before they had really caught up with the United States, even in terms of per capita income.

Over the last twenty-five years it has proven difficult or impossible for capitalism to adapt its social base to the requirements of development. In this we can see a real decadence in the historical formation, decadence not in the frequently nebulous sense of a value crisis, but rather in the specific sense that the development of the productive forces makes the capitalist system ever more concentrated and abstract, and therefore restricts its social base. The system tries to compensate for this through new policies but does not succeed in doing so in a stable fashion. This is a decadence that is different from past manifestations, in the sense that capitalism needs to undertake specific subjective initiatives to broaden its social base but always lags behind needs.

IL MANIFESTO: What are you referring to, specifically?

AMIN: I'm thinking, for example, about the Italian Communist Party's "historical compromise" in Italy, which came—which became possible—not in 1964, when it would have averted 1968, but with a lag of almost ten years, and which was therefore destined to failure and to aggravate the capitalist crisis. To take an example from the past, I am thinking of the Roman emperors who became Christians, but at least a century too late to save the empire.

IL MANIFESTO: Do you mean that it's a matter of salvaging something and not of exercising hegemony?

AMIN: Exactly. We are in a situation where capitalism has lost its capacity for initiative, but where the working class does not currently have the initiative either. All this does not mean *Zusammenbruch,* automatic breakdown, and so forth because capitalism can always get out of its crises.

IL MANIFESTO: We agree in general terms about the crisis, but how, in what form, by what means do you think that capitalism can emerge from it? What are the system's predictable responses?

FRANK: In the discussion to which we referred at the beginning, we arrived at hypotheses about alternative models of later capitalism. Each of these models would be the result of the evolution of the class struggle, of the system's "spontaneous" tendencies, of its subjective reactions, and so on. Obviously, capitalism could also try pure resistance: for example, a certain degree of development of social consumption could possibly serve as a palliative, but *only* as a palliative. I am thinking, for example, about public transportation and restructuring urban facilities: something like this was done in the United States after the 1920s, and it is no accident that Fiat and Volkswagen are investing in subway projects.

IL MANIFESTO: But collective consumption could not become a new motor force for capitalist development.

FRANK: Certainly not. In addition, we must make it very clear that our three alternative models for capitalist emergence from the crisis are located in the context of Orwell's *1984*—we have even called them "1984, Numbers One, Two, and Three."

AMIN: Let us begin with the first one and describe what a state of equilibrium might be for the new accumulation model. It will cause a deep transformation of the international division of labor, with a transfer of the mass of productive activities to the periphery and the development of the new leading sectors in the center: technology, atomic and solar energy, appropriation of marine, biochemical, and genetic resources, and so on.

IL MANIFESTO: In sum, in the United States there will only be highly qualified technicians and the workers will be concentrated in the Congo?

AMIN: There are many intermediate positions between the United States and the Congo, and this model—of subimperialism—would lead to extreme accentuation of unequal development. But all this requires a long parenthesis about what we mean by subimperialism.

FRANK: Our two main theses involve development based on subimperialism and development based on the exacerbation of the current situation. The third thesis lies between these two.

AMIN: Because of its monopoly of technology, the center would have a concentration of key industries and overall control of the productive system. As a corollary, the classical industrial apparatus would be transferred to the periphery, but it would be an unequal transfer, polarized at several points. The countries in which the classical industrial apparatus would be concentrated would export industrial products to the center and to other regions of the periphery, while importing technology from the center and raw materials from other countries on the periphery. When these mechanisms have reached a certain quantitative level, there will also be qualitative changes within individual nations. Individual bourgeoisies, submissive to outside technological domination, will need to develop their own strong social base and, therefore, nationalist tendencies vis-à-vis other underdeveloped countries. On this basis, they would try to win alliances with social strata that would be potential allies of a revolutionary movement. This is what is taking place in subimperialist areas, and we should not underestimate it. In this context it is clear that the subjective political aspects of individual bourgeoisies becomes important.

IL MANIFESTO: This subimperialist development scheme, and the model of the international division of labor which it implies, lets the countries with postwar miracles—Western Europe and Japan—become the nerve centers of the crisis. They are the ones that will suffer from competition from decentralized industrial production, without having the strength to become metropoles.

AMIN: Before getting to that point, we must focus our attention on the kind of equilibrium that is possible between this model of accumulation and the system of class alliances which could be formed at the national and international levels. It is in this delicate balance and the contradictions it implies that we can identify the space for possible revolutionary advance. First of all, there will be a notable reduction in productive employment in the center, although for the moment we cannot see who will be better off and who will be worse off. (In addition, there has already been a decrease in the relative weight of the working class in the classical sense in the capitalist countries.) This means a stage where there will be tension over employment and wage problems. But this decrease in directly productive employment implies stronger pressure on the employed—especially those employed in classical industry and consequently in the periphery—to obtain the surplus with which to support, in diverse ways, those parasitical layers which tend to be more numerous. This is not equally easy everywhere.

In the second phase, for this model to function it is necessary that the ruling class in the subimperialist countries (the bureaucratic or private bourgeoisies) succeed in broadening its base of support to include strata that are socially opposed to submission to imperialism, and this is not easy either. Finally, this model implies a countercoup in a much more proletarianized periphery and in the center as well (in the form of guest workers), and therefore the extension of a sort of apartheid in both the center and the periphery—the creation of new slaves of the system. Typical of this system would be an equally high degree of productivity, but this equality would nonetheless correspond to an extraordinary diversity of treatment.

FRANK: It would be the South Africanization of the world, which we call "1984 Number One," with generalized racism and a very strong social and political hierarchy.

IL MANIFESTO: According to this South Africanization model, would large-scale parasitism in the advanced areas provide the market outlet for industrial production in the periphery?

AMIN: Yes. There would be an apparent upheaval in the current division of labor, with high technology and perhaps even raw materials or pseudo-raw materials—atomic and solar energy, the petroliferous slate in Canada, all the kinds of raw materials which up to now the industrialized areas have procured by sacking the natural resources of the periphery—being provided by the advanced areas. A sort of transformation of the mechanism.

FRANK: And the production of these pseudo-raw materials becomes feasible and possible precisely because of the oil price rise.

AMIN: It could perhaps function through this mechanism—I am more optimistic than Gunder—but only in the two extremes of the system, among the great powers and in the poorest areas which lack any kind of political defense. For the whole intermediate area, which is enormous and includes almost all of Europe and a good half of the Third World, conditions would be extremely tense and unstable. That is where the weak links of the chain are located.

They are weak links because in those areas the kind of restructuring of social alliances which would have to be imposed is one which the ruling classes have not achieved even during periods of rapid growth. In this area, violent struggles would be unleashed among the different national bourgeoisies, each one of which would attempt to compensate at the expense of its own proletariat. Major tensions and the possibility of revolutionary breaks would line the path of South Africanization. The renewed strength of the United States, as a result of the oil crisis and the antiproletarian reaction of the weakest industrialized countries, might be a foreshadowing of major conflict. Moreover, in these intermediate areas the different bourgeoisies are having even more trouble restructuring their own social bases because of the current crisis: under present conditions it seems crazy to the ruling groups of the Italian bourgeoisie to abandon the urban alliance in exchange for the less-than-secure neutrality of the proletariat and Communist Party. In addition, the potential subimperialisms must clear the way themselves, thus producing new conflicts.

Even at the top, this will not be an easy operation. In the United States, a violent conflict has already begun between multinationals (which would be the victors in the South Africanization model) and those industries that produce for the domestic market and would be the losers. (In my opinion, Watergate was a warning of this.) This kind of problem characteristically shows up before the model begins functioning. A truly revolutionary period is thus beginning, with nerve centers spread throughout the intermediate areas. In this context one can cite the example of India, whose bourgeoisie was able to broaden its base of support precisely because of its integration into the world market; now it is being strangled because of the oil crisis and its effect on the balance of payments.

FRANK: According to estimates which seem exaggerated to me, India would have to spend 80 percent of its foreign currency—opposed to 10–11 percent at this moment—to assure oil imports.

AMIN: The situation is being turned around. Integration of the world capitalist system, which was the condition for broadening the social base of the Indian bourgeoisie, is what is now provoking this brutal restriction.

FRANK: Let's move on to the other model. Together with the one based on a new division of labor and the generalization of racism, there is the possibility of a second model which, in substance, is an exacerbation of the current situation. No racism, and nothing new of importance in the international division of labor, in the sense that a new international division of labor would not develop alongside a realignment between new and old industrial sectors. In place of that there would be the greatest possible concentration of the productive apparatus in the United States, Europe, and Japan. This would be model "1984 Number Two." "1984 Number Three" would have this concentration in the center, with some crumbs for the periphery and the establishment of some mini-subimperialisms. The second model presupposes a regime of total social repression in the metropole, which will be particularly harsh during the restructuring phase.

IL MANIFESTO: Nonetheless, such a model would not involve a contraction of the productive base in the center.

AMIN: No. No contraction of the productive base, and even relative growth once it was put in place. But it will require at least twenty years to put it in place: to use more productive technology, readjust the labor force, and reconstruct a wage hierarchy. During that time all the myths and ideologies which have marked the last twenty-five years of development will go under. In broad outline, it would be a repetition of the 1914–1945 period: a revolution, fascism and Nazism, two world wars. From the moment that traditional industry is not transferred to outside areas with low wages, as in this model, the cost of financing the restructuring will have to be shouldered by the working class employed in the traditional industries in the central countries.

FRANK: Supposing an equilibrium situation for this model is possible, it is politically very difficult to achieve, difficult enough to make us believe that this model could not come into being. The situation we are in today is the result of twenty-five years of continuous expansion. The way out of it, new markets, a new 1945, must come from the destruction of the current productive apparatus.

AMIN: All this brings repression along with it, and not repression of the fascist type, if by fascism we understand a class alliance between the industrial-financial bourgeoisie and intermediate strata belonging to earlier stages of development. It would be the real 1984: one-dimensional order, violent repression of minorities, together with a diffuse liberalism—in short, repressive tolerance.

IL MANIFESTO: Going back to the first hypothesis, that of the international division of labor, it seems to us that this would require an Atlantic-type solution—in other words, the greatest possible coordination among countries in the center. Only given a hypothetical general agreement could the traditional industrial apparatus of the developed countries be redistributed to the periphery. But, in your opinion, is the likelihood one of maximum agreement or maximum conflict?

AMIN: In my opinion, maximum conflict, a struggle breaking out among the different clans of the bourgeoisie. And we have to take into account the fact that a policy involving subimperialist countries is already beginning. Moreover, this seems to me to be the dominant tendency in recent years: confrontation in monetary and tariff areas, confrontation within the European Economic Community, confrontations among the different powers to insure their control over Egypt, Mauritania, or Tunisia.

IL MANIFESTO: In fact, a consideration of the three hypothetical responses you attribute to the system leads us to concentrate our attention on the ways in which they would be carried out. This seems to be a long road, marked by acute social and international conflicts and with no brilliant solutions. After a crisis and a violence-ridden process we will still arrive at 1984-type solutions: racism and South Africanization or one-dimensional order and systematic repression. We can conclude from that, that the more abstract capitalism becomes, the more monsters it produces. But as we understood it, you formulated these abstract models mainly to show the problems involved in putting them into effect, the conflicts they engender, and the spaces that can be opened up.

Before moving on to the third point, we would be interested in having your opinion on the topic of the day: inflation and the oil crisis.

AMIN: There has been a great deal of political use made of the oil crisis. Of course the price of oil and raw materials has risen, but in the industrialized world the inflation levels were already high before this crisis, as a result of a redistribution of domestic income. Moreover, the fact that the price of crude oil has doubled does not have an enormous effect, inasmuch as the price of crude makes up 10 percent of the final price of oil. To impute the 15 percent rise in the cost of living to oil is absurd.

FRANK: Insofar as a prohibition on Sunday driving or the reduction of television scheduling will have no effect on the balance-of-payments problem, it seems to me that the only reason for the austerity measures that have been adopted is to make a favorable atmosphere for repression. 1984 is not only a figment of our imagination. Moreover, regarding inflation, my position is very simple: inflation happens when profits fall, to put a brake on the fall, and this is relatively easy in an economy where monopoly groups have a strong presence.

IL MANIFESTO: We have now reached our fourth question on the crisis. This is the hypothesis that the current international crisis marks a particular stage: capitalism's entry into a phase in which its historical function has been used up, the function Marx attributes to it in a few pages of the *Manifesto*. More specifically, because capitalism is unable to satisfy society's needs, even those needs it contributed to creating, the need for and timeliness of going beyond it become apparent.

FRANK: Each capitalist crisis has normally resulted in restructuring, the scope of which has been proportional to the seriousness of the crisis. For precisely this reason, we have emphasized the fact that a long period of crisis is awaiting us, which will see profound and dramatic conflicts. Inasmuch as capital is historical, it could happen that at the end of the tunnel capitalist development does not recover. I do not believe that capitalism has reached the end of its history.

AMIN: I would answer your last question affirmatively and with conviction, and I would even refer to a specific date: 1917. 1917 shows us that for the first time in its history, capitalism did not have what was required to resolve a certain number of problems of human society. From that moment on, it began to be evident that its historical function of accumulation and the liberation of people from their submission to nature had been exhausted. The fact that the USSR's problems were subsequently badly resolved, that the October Revolution had a particular outcome, in no way cancels out this proof of capitalism's historic incapacity. Really, one could say that the Sovet mode of production has in fact resolved problems in the USSR that capitalism was not able to resolve. In this sense, the Soviet mode of production also marks the beginning of a transition phase, not the triumphal and brilliant one envisaged by Stalinism, but nevertheless a transition. All over the world, more and more problems accumulate every day that capitalism cannot resolve, constantly reinforcing the need to go beyond capitalism.

IL MANIFESTO: This does not imply the inevitability of its downfall—much less its total collapse?

AMIN: Exhaustion of its historical function does not imply the inability to further develop the productive forces. But that is not the point we are discussing. To go back to a parallel which seems useful to me as long as it remains a parallel, to the end of its existence the Roman Empire continued to be superior to the barbarians at all levels—technical, military, and administrative. This did not negate the fact that it was already in a decadent phase, meaning that it had exhausted its historical function and had shown itself to be less and less capable of responding to the needs and problems which grew out of the social conflicts of those centuries. Moreover, to return to our own case, what other meaning do our different formulations of 1984 have? We have set up abstractions of possible and coherent capitalist solutions to the current crisis, but we have done so in order to show the barbarism of the solution, and, even more, to show the impracticality of the road that would take us from today's reality to that of 1984. In this sense capitalism must be said to have exhausted its historical function.

IL MANIFESTO: We are in overall, though incomplete, agreement with everything you attribute to 1917 and, as a consequence, to the current crisis. Undoubtedly, 1917 represented a change, not only because it revealed capitalism's inability to resolve the problems of a part of humanity, but also because it demonstrated that the capitalist system, left to its own logic, would lead to catastrophic results: generalized wars, fascism, repression. But it is also a proven fact that after the break in 1917 the capitalist system placed constraints on its logic and succeeded in giving new impetus to its development and its hegemony as well—to the point that it was even able to reabsorb, either wholly or in part, movements which had represented anticapitalist breaks. At bottom it is the experience of World War II and the twenty-five years of development that followed; we have experienced not only a new growth push but also new momentum for the system's credibility and the credibility of some of its values. In this respect the 1917 rupture seems to us to be a predecessor of the current crisis. This crisis is not a linear consequence of that break; rather, it represents a new trend, which does not mean a choice between revolution and catastrophe in the next ten—even thirty—years. And this trend shows up when capitalism's incapacity is no longer limited to some of the problems of one part of humanity but extends to all of the problems pertaining to all of humanity.

It seems to us that for the first time in its history, capitalist development is no longer being proposed as a satisfactory model, even by relatively privileged social strata and countries. In the second place, it is also the first time that needs and social struggles raise the demand for new relations of production so clearly. In more explicit terms, this is the first time that the demand for a new historical formation which is not based on the division of labor and the delegation of power has arisen so widely and without utopian connotations. This is the point where the struggle of the proletariat can no longer be contained within the categories of capitalist development and becomes a demand for a different way of organizing production.

AMIN: I agree completely. It is no accident that the system's responses, which have become increasingly abstract, fit into a "1984" perspective, the same one that Orwell described, based on fragments of US society and Hitlerism. I recently re-read *The German Ideology* and found a sentence which I underlined repeatedly, the one which affirms that communism is necessary if humankind is to avoid total destruction. This, and nothing else, seems to me to be the meaning of the famous "socialism or barbarism" dilemma: to hammer home the need for communism as the only historical possible way for resolving the problems capitalist development has posed for contemporary humanity. And in this sense, Marx's hypothesis that capitalism succeeds in creating the historical subject capable of overcoming it—in other words, its own tomb—holds. The most negative aspect of the 1984 perspective would be precisely the destruction of the proletariat as the highest productive force and antagonist class: the proletarianization of everyone and the end of the proletariat. But there are no two straight roads from here either to 1984 or to communism, rather a sort of contradiction, in which we must pay a great deal of attention to internal contradictions in the dominant forces which tend to be accentuated by the crisis. Let us not forget that the Russian and Chinese proletariats won because the institutions of power were disintegrating, because the dominant forces were divided.

In conclusion, with each step the political tendency to conserve power by moving toward 1984, thus remaining within the capitalist system, provokes reactions that could reverse the tendency and begin a revolutionary process. These reactions, these countertendencies, show up in both the center and the periphery, but I believe they are most likely in the so-called central fringe: the advanced parts of the periphery and backward parts of the center. This is the area where contradictions will be the most concentrated and where the greatest potential for an alternative will lie.

IL MANIFESTO: In this context, do you attribute an important role to the countries of the periphery and the process of proletarianization which is taking place?

AMIN: It has never been a mystery to me that the United States should be the country closest to 1984. It is no accident, but the result of a series of historical circumstances. The existence of a civilization built on immigration and, especially, the lack of a past, the lack of a precapitalist base, explains the rapid growth of the United States. But it also makes it a backward country, where proletarian consciousness remains at a very low level. Unlike other countries in the West—and this is important—the links were never created between the Chinese Cultural Revolution and the deepest demands of the working class for egalitarianism and against the division of labor. This is an embryonic phenomenon, but it indicates the tendency toward consolidation of anticapitalist impulses. This tendency is strongest in the industrialized areas of Japan and Europe (with internal differences, because in my opinion southern Europe exhibits important peculiarities) and in advanced areas of the periphery.

I do not entirely agree with you when you say that protest

against the division of labor has arisen only in recent years with the Chinese Cultural Revolution. This protest was first expressed by the utopian socialists at the time of the industrial revolution and the birth of capitalism and reappeared with the Paris Commune. I want to stress this in order to put forward a thesis, albeit a risky and certainly not exhaustive one, which supports the possibility of a consolidation between areas of old capitalism, advanced areas in the periphery, and processes of proletarianization on an international scale. In effect, I attribute a great deal of importance to the vestiges of barter (exchange based on use value) which are still present in some areas of the metropolis (not in the United States) and in the advanced peripheries and among the millions of people who have recently become part of the proletariat. At this point in the crisis of capitalism's historical function (and therefore of its culture as well, a culture based on exchange value), the system's inability to solve problems of growing importance for humanity could produce a positive response, or the basis for a positive response, out of this memory of use value. Today this is no longer a critique coming from romantics (and from utopian socialists or reactionaries); rather it is a true alternative political struggle, a rejection of the 1984 perspective, a way out of the system toward the creation of a new social formation. To say that this prospect can exist means that we must look for it: to wait only means to wait for 1984.

NOTES

1. Paul A. Samuelson, in *The Business Cycle Today,* ed. V. Zarnovitz (Washington: National Bureau of Economic Research, 1970), p. 167.
2. Alexander Eckstein in ibid.
3. Solomon Fabricant in ibid., p. 4.
4. Kermit Gordon, "Some Conjectures on Policy Problems of the 1970's," *American Economic Review,* May 1975.
5. Geoffrey Moore, "Some Secular Changes in Business Cycles," *American Economic Review,* May 1974, pp. 133–135.
6. Robert L. Heilbroner, "Proceedings of the Annual Meetings of the American Economic Association," December 28–30, 1973, *American Economic Review,* May 1974.
7. Joseph S. Davis, *The World Between the Wars. 1919–1939: An Economist's View* (Baltimore, 1975), pp. 394, 398.
8. Ibid., p. 194.
9. J. Jewkes, quoted in ibid., p. 406.
10. Joseph A. Schumpeter, *Business Cycles,* vol. 2 (New York, 1939), pp. 793–794.
11. For a depressing but revealing catalogue of continuous misprediction, misdiagnosis, and refusal to see the reality before their eyes in this period, see John Kenneth Galbraith, *The Great Crash, 1929* (Boston, 1961).
12. Walter W. Heller, "What's Right With Economics?" Presidential address delivered to the AEA on December 29, 1974, published in the *American Economic Review,* March 1975.
13. Ibid.
14. Paul A. Samuelson, *Economics: An Introductory Analysis,* 4th ed. (New York, 1958).
15. Mark Blaug, "Kuhn Versus Lakatos, or Paradigms Versus Research Programmes in the History of Economics," *History of Political Economy,* vol. 7, no. 4, 1975.
16. Joseph Steindl, *Maturity and Stagnation in American Capitalism* (New York: Monthly Review Press, 1976).
17. Paul A. Baran and Paul M. Sweezy, *Monopoly Capital* (New York: Monthly Review Press, 1966).

18. Moore, "Some Secular Changes in Business Cycles," p. 135.

19. Richard C. Edwards, "The Impact of Industrial Concentration on Inflation and the Economic Crisis," in *Radical Perspectives on the Economic Crisis of Monopoly Capitalism* (New York: Union of Radical Political Economics, 1975); Howard Sherman, "Inflation, Unemployment and Monopoly Capital," *Monthly Review,* vol. 27, no. 10, 1976.

20. Sherman in ibid., pp. 32–33.

21. Roger Bratenstein, "First Steps Towards a Cyclical Theory for LDC's," *Intereconomics,* October 1974.

22. Quoted in Edwards, "The Impact of Industrial Concentration," p. 44.

23. Quoted in David Gordon, "Capital vs. Labor: The Current Crisis in the Sphere of Production," in *Radical Perspectives on the Economic Crisis of Monopoly Capitalism* (New York: Union of Radical Political Economics, 1975), p. 34.

24. Gottfried Haberler, *Weltwirtschaftliches Archiv,* vol. 2 (Kiel, 1974), p. 191.

25. Ibid., pp. 182, 184.

26. Paul M. Sweezy and Harry Magdoff, *The Dynamics of U.S. Capitalism,* (New York: Monthly Review Press, 1972), pp. 172–173.

27. Charles P. Kindleberger, *The World Depression, 1929–1939* (Berkeley, 1973).

28. Fred Block, "Contradictions of Capitalism as a World System," *Insurgent Sociologist,* vol. 1, no. 2, 1975, pp. 10–12.